Contents

KU-735-180

Contents

A REVIEW OF READING TESTS

A critical review of reading tests and assess-ment procedures available for use in British schools.

By Denis Vincent, Len Green, Jean Francis and Janet Powney

With contributions by:

Carla Broderick
Jenny Davies
Janet Henney
Chris Lewis
Gwilym Scourfield
Vera Quin

NFER-NELSON

Published by The NFER-NELSON Publishing Company Ltd.,
Darville House, 2 Oxford Road East,
Windsor, Berks. SL4 1DF.

First Published 1983
© Denis Vincent, Len Green, Jean Francis and Janet Powney
ISBN 0-7005-1000-1
Code 8147 02 1

Photoset by FD Graphics Limited, Fleet, Hampshire.
Printed in Great Britain.

Distributed in the USA by Humanities Press Inc.,
Atlantic Highlands, New Jersey 07716 USA

Introduction

This book reviews, test-by-test, published reading tests and assessment procedures currently available to British schools in 1982/3. It is intended as an initial reference and guide to aid selection of new tests or evaluate tests already in use. Reviews are addressed primarily to 'consumers', both in schools and LEAs, rather than to test researchers or constructers.

The reviews discuss content, purpose and technical features and offer brief critical appraisals. They are not a substitute for publishers' catalogues or specimen/ inspection copies. These should also be consulted before final decisions about purchase and use.

This guide could have been restricted to standardized tests of the type reviewed in Section I, following. This would have presented an excessively narrow (and depressing) view of reading assessment, concentrated upon its role in administration rather than in teaching. Options for the latter use are diverse, ranging from diagnostic, clinical and criterion-referenced tests to checklists and, ultimately, full-length books on diagnostic teaching. Examples of such materials are reviewed in Section II. Considerable problems of inclusion criteria were encountered in selecting material for this section and certain arbitrary limits had to be drawn. Full-length books were excluded, as were most materials unavailable in the UK and tests of oral vocabulary, listening and 'English' lacking an explicit reading component. This left a heterogeneous selection of 'instruments' (tests and procedures) differing in technical basis and in purpose and approach to reading. Final selection was made to present teachers with a comprehensive, but not exhaustive, 'shop window' of options. Most of these are reviewed, without attempt at sub-categorization, in Section II. A sub-group, clearly identifiable as 'checklists' is reviewed in Section III. Finally, Section IV reviews a number of procedures for assessing spelling.

THE REVIEWS

As far as possible the reviews follow a standard form, headed by a list of main features, condensed to save space and avoid tedious repetition in the text:

Group/Individual. (Most group tests can also be administered individually.)

Objective. A test is classed as objective if scoring does not require subjective/impressionistic judgement. Often this means automatic right/wrong scoring but it includes identification of oral reading errors.

Standardized/Unstandardized. A test is classed as 'standardized' if scores can be scaled to relate performance to a standard or average level referred to as a 'norm'.

Age Group for Test. This is usually given as a chronological age in years and months (e.g. ten years and eight months would be represented as 10.08) and may be based on the age range for which tests are standardized, author's recommendations or, if necessary, on the reviewer's own judgement. Further direct reference to test materials is always advisable.

Score Conversion Scales. Most standardized tests use 'Reading Ages' or 'Standardized Scores'. Their interpretation is usually clearly explained in an accompanying manual.

Timed/Untimed. Exact time-allowance are given if a test is timed. Otherwise an approximation may be given. It is worth noting that longer tests may require more than one testing session. The administrative inconvenience absenteeism can cause in such cases should not be underestimated.

Equivalent Forms. Where there are equivalent or parallel versions available the number of these is given in parentheses.

Consumable/Re-usable. This is intended to give some indication of how far test materials such as record forms or answer books can only be used once. It is sometimes only a rough guide as some tests have both re-usable and disposable or consumable parts. Re-usable materials have obvious economic advantages, particularly when long-term routine use is intended. However, reviews do not include details of the price of test materials although there is sometimes a general reference to implications of cost. Publishers' own catalogues are much better suited to take account of price changes and discounts and to provide space to itemize prices of each component in more elaborate tests.

Country of Origin. Some reading tests were developed outside the UK although they are not necessarily unsuitable for British children. Unfortunately there are some tests distributed in the UK which seem to be obsolete remainders of large print runs in the USA.

Most reviews commence with reference to the purpose of the test. This always reflects the stated or implied intentions of the test author and should not be regarded as reviewer's recommendations. An outline description of the test itself follows and as far as possible this is based on the latest version. The aim is to give an *impression* of the activities involved. Some tests would be hard to describe clearly without inclusion of unwieldy examples.

Wherever appropriate some comment is made upon the technical qualities of the test. Three main features are usually considered:

Reliability. This is a statistical index which shows how far test results are subject to error or chance fluctuations. This may be done by giving the same test (or equivalent forms) twice to the same children and correlating the two sets of results – 'test-retest' reliability.

Alternatively, a statistical analysis may be performed on a single set of results to give an 'internal-consistency' reliability. This is usually given as the 'KR20' or 'KR21' value. However obtained, the reliability index shows how far the test falls short of 'perfect' reliability – expressed as 1.0. Reading tests rarely exceed a reliability of .98 although few published examples have inadequate reliabilities.

Validity. This is most typically expressed as a correlation between the test and some other criterion, often another reading test, although the concept of validity is more subtle than this would imply. In general terms it refers to the evidence that the test measures what it claims to measure. In the case of reading this raises some formidable psychological, philosophical and curricular issues which can only be touched upon in the reviews.

Standardization. Where norms are provided for tests it is desirable that these are fairly recent – some tests were standardized over 20 years ago –

and based on a relevant sample of children. Ideally the sample should be designed to reflect a stated national – or regional – age group. In practice tests vary greatly in the extent to which they meet such criteria.

The above are the technical or 'psychometric' criteria by which reading tests have conventionally been judged and reviews take due account of them.

Numerous texts on educational assessment explain them in greater detail and these should be consulted by anyone who is unfamiliar with the above concepts. However, it may be that excessive prestige has been attached to these. Most reviews endeavour to give equal or greater weight to other criteria in the final evaluation. These include practical considerations, the soundness of the model of reading behind the test and the test's potential to contribute constructively to teaching.

The majority of the reviews were prepared by the editorial group. Further contributions were made by individuals with particular interest or expertise in certain tests or where an independent opinion was required. Overall, the reviews reflect a variety of theoretical and practical perspectives. It would not have been practical to evaluate all review tests in actual field trials. Inevitably, much use was made of theoretical and academic judgement and consultation with teachers who had used particular tests. It would be useful to have had even more information from the latter source and the editors would welcome written evaluations by users of any of the tests reviewed. These would be taken account of in preparing any up-dated or revised edition of this volume. (Address for correspondence, Editors, *Review of Reading Tests,* School of Education and Humanities, North East London Polytechnic, Longbridge Road, Dagenham RM8 2AS.)

Section I: Attainment Tests

The tests reviewed in this Section are all standardized measures of reading attainment. That is, they assess the reader's ability relative to a 'norm' – the standard or average for readers of a specific age group. A test is said to be standardized if norms have been established by administering the test to a sample, usually a large one, of children who are representative of their age group.

Most of the tests give a general or global measure of reading ability based on the child's total 'raw' score – the number of questions ('items') correctly answered or words correctly read. In a number of tests a further distinction is made between separate sections or 'sub-tests'. These contribute to a profile of performance in different skills or aspects of reading.

Tests usually have at least two components. The most basic group tests are comprised of a **test booklet** containing the items and a **manual** of instructions for the teacher. As an elaboration there may be some form of **separate answer sheet** so test booklets can be re-used, a separate **scoring key** or **template** to facilitate marking and separate class or individual **record forms.** Individual tests tend to be simpler, usually comprising a re-usable **test card** or **reading booklet,** a **manual** and, possibly, a **record form.** Separate test components are identified in bold face when first mentioned in the text of a review.

It will become apparent in reading these reviews that many of the tests are regarded with, at best, lukewarm enthusiasm by their reviewers. There are certainly some poor tests available to assess reading attainment. Sadly, they are not also the least widely used. Nevertheless, some positive options do exist and these are clearly signalled by certain reviews.

The Bowman Test of Reading Competence

Anthony J. Bowers and Margaret Mann

1980

SRA

Group; Objective; Standardized; 7.10 – 10.09; Quotients (standardized scores), Reading Ages, T-Scores; Untimed (20 minutes); Consumable; UK.

The Bowman is a 65-item cloze procedure test using four prose passages. No specific uses for the test are suggested, but it would be suitable for the usual purposes associated with a global measure of comprehension ability. Also, items are classified as 'Syntactic' or 'Semantic' according to whether the deleted words convey meaning or serve a primarily grammatical function. This allows sub-scores to be calculated – implying a diagnostic application. However, these sub-scores were found by the test authors to be highly intercorrelated (.79 to .90) and cannot be regarded as measuring psychologically separate dimensions of language.

The test passages are ranked in order of readability according to Fry's Readability Chart with passage reading age levels from 6.00 years to 12.00 years. The style of the prose is straightforward, if not bland. It seems likely that the passages were written especially for the test. Deletions are systematic to take account of various features of the passages, rather than random. Page-size **marking templates** accompany the test. These locate the items in windows, next to which the correct answers are specified, together with the Semantic or Syntactic categorization of the item. Generally, only one response is specified as correct. A **class record sheet** accompanies the test with columns for names, scores and significant differences between sub-scores.

The seven-page **Manual** briefly reviews the rationale of cloze procedure, mentioning possible enrichment activities based on cloze, and gives the usual administration instructions, conversion tables and notes on construction. This brevity may be appreciated by potential users although there are occasional ambiguities which might have been avoided in a longer account. For example, fuller details of standardization would have been welcomed and the discussion of standard error of measurement needs careful reading before it is clear that it refers to pupils' raw scores.

Reading ages for the test range from 7.08 to 11.01 and standardized scores with age adjustment are tabulated for the 7.10 to 10.09 range. The sub-scores are converted to T-Scores (with a mean of 50 and one point of score equal to a tenth of a standard deviation) and a supplementary table gives the size of Semantic/Syntactic T-Score differences statistically significant at various age levels. Reliability is high (.95 test-retest, .94 internal consistency). Validity studies of correlations with the *SPAR Test* (q.v.) and with teachers' ratings of pupils are reported. Respective values of .86 and a median value of .78 were found in these. A sample of 2,393 junior children, drawn from 25 schools in eight LEAs was used for standardization. It would appear that some general criteria were employed to obtain a representative cross-section of schools. Technically, the Bowman is certainly not inferior to other standardized cloze procedure tests although the creation of equivalent forms would have been desirable.

This test is of some interest as a first attempt to incorporate a sub-score system into a standardized cloze test. There have been claims for the 'diagnostic' potential of cloze procedure, but there is still little direct evidence for it. Most studies of the psychological structure of cloze have shown that the items all measure the 'same thing' however much the deleted words vary linguistically. This is clearly the case with the Syntactic and Semantic sub-scores of the Bowman Test. Its current appeal rests mainly upon the recency of standardization, convenience of marking and freedom from the idiosyncrasies which flaw some other published cloze tests.

The Burt Word Reading Test (1974 Revision)

Scottish Council for Research in Education

1980

Hodder & Stoughton

Individual; Objective; Standardized; 6.04–12.00; Reading Ages; Untimed (approximately 10 minutes); Re-usable; UK.

This 1974 revision is a new version of the *Burt (Rearranged) Word Reading Test* which is now out of print. The latest version presents a re-ordering of some of the words in accordance with changes in the relative difficulties found in the course of the standardization.

The test consists of 110 words printed on a **test card** and graded in approximate order of difficulty. The child is told to read as many words as he can, at his own speed. He continues until he has attempted and failed at least four consecutive words. It is then presumed that the remainder are too difficult for him, but he is allowed to look ahead and pick out any other words he thinks he can manage. From the total number of words which he can correctly decode without aid his reading age can be immediately calculated using the table of norms provided.

The 16-page **Manual** gives clear directions for applying the test, as well as details of the standardization. The latter is based on a study of a representative group of 2,000 Scottish primary school children. The test reliability is high (KR20 = .97).

The Bullock Report revealed that the previous version of the Burt test was being used in one third of all primary schools and in fifteen per cent of secondary schools. It would appear that the sheer popularity of the test prompted the Scottish Council for Research in Education to undertake the latest revision – the decision can hardly have been based on any other virtues of the test!

Class teachers should note that the reading age norms should not be used in the first year of the junior school and that they are of restricted utility in the second year as well. However, the Manual does explain how class norms may be used for all stages of the junior school. The norms are based on a representative sample of Scottish children and may differ from particular localities in England and Wales. The most recently reported set of local norms in England are those for Cheshire. (See SHEARER, E. and APPS, R. (1975) *Educational Research*, 18,1.)

Despite the criticisms which have been levelled at the 'shortness and simplicity' of the test it clearly has a special appeal to class teachers, especially for the ease with which raw scores can be converted to reading ages. The test does not claim to assess fluency and comprehension skills. However, it has the advantage of being given individually and as such it may help in the preliminary diagnosis of the child with reading difficulties; e.g. in the type of errors he makes. Nevertheless, the Manual stresses that other and more specific tests are required to identify the problem faced by this type of child.

The appeal of the Burt, and indeed its companion *Schonell Graded Word Reading Test* (q.v.), is largely economic rather than educational. Reading, even in the early stages, is essentially concerned with getting meaning from the printed word, yet, to give the Burt is to impose an intrinsically meaningless task upon a child. It is therefore important that users of the test are clear in their own minds that the immediate practical advantages of its use outweigh more profound adverse considerations.

Cloze Reading Tests

D. Young

1982

Hodder & Stoughton

Group; Objective; Standardized; 8.00–12.06; Quotients (standardized scores), Reading Ages (7.00 – 15.06); Timed, 35 minutes; 3 compatible levels; Consumable; UK.

Young describes cloze procedure as a measure of reading skills that makes use of, but transcends, recognition of printed forms and the knowledge of the meaning of words. Essentially, these tests provide standardized measures of reading comprehension suited to the same uses as other standardized attainment tests.

There are three levels of the test. Each is printed as a separate booklet. It is suggested Level 1 is used for second-year and early third-year juniors, Level 2 for the second half of the second-year and third- and fourth-year juniors, and Level 3 for the second half of the third year, the fourth year and in the first part of the first secondary year. Each Level contains 70 items presented over a graded series of short, unrelated passages containing between two and six blanks in which the missing words are to be written. The first two passages are common to all three levels, thereafter the material has been designed to match the ability range of the intended year groups.

The administrative procedure is standard to allow more than one level to be used in group testing so that classes of mixed ability may be tested in the same room. The **Manual** provides separate conversion tables for each level of the test and gives a convenient rule-of-thumb for equating scores on different versions. In addition to age-adjusted standardized scores for the 8.00–12.06 age range, reading ages are provided: Level 1, 7.00–13.01; Level 2, 7.01–14.03; Level 3, 7.04–15.06. However, these extensions beyond the standardized score range were obtained using small samples, and are intended only as a rough guide. The main standardization was based on over 900 children for each level. These appear to have been drawn from an 'opportunity sample' of schools, rather than a conventionally-selected national sample. However, evidence is presented to suggest the sample was adequate for the purpose of producing norms for the tests. It should also be noted that the standardized score conversion tables cover a wider age range than that reported for the standardization sample. This suggests that the tables may have been 'stretched' by eight months at the lower end of the age range and ten months at the upper. Such 'extrapolation' beyond the age range actually tested assumes a consistent linear trend for score to increase with age. As a rough guideline this is reasonable although to apply it over ten months of age from 11.08 to 12.06 may involve applying a 'steeper' rate of progress with age than is really the case.

Internal consistency reliability values of .937, .936 and .931 are quoted for the three levels, and validity, in the form of correlations with other reading and spelling tests, is adequately demonstrated.

The individual test passages are written in a clear, if rather bland, contemporary prose style. However, this neutrality of style, and the relative brevity of the passages means that some of the more sophisticated inferential aspects of reading are probably excluded from the tests. Also, the content of the passages is strongly male-oriented. Where the sex of a character is revealed it is invariably male and there are no references to girls or women. In a test of such recent origin a greater balance in content might have been expected. There is also an imbalance in the choice of items. It is striking that the majority of the words deleted are structural rather than semantic in function. They are, for the most part, articles, conjunctions, pronouns and verb auxiliaries which could be guessed correctly solely by reference to the grammatical structure of their surrounding sentences with little reference to meaning or overall context. In this respect, The Cloze Reading Tests are disappointingly trivial applications of cloze procedure. The author's introductory remarks about reading creatively and the 'search for meaning' which 'dominates what is presented by the page' seem distinctly hollow in view of the prevalence of 'the', 'is', 'were' and 'to' as deleted words.

Edinburgh Reading Tests, Stage 1

**The Godfrey Thomson Unit,
University of Edinburgh**

1977

Hodder & Stoughton

Group; Objective; Standardized; 7.00–9.00; Reading
Ages, Quotients (age-adjusted standardized scores),
Standardized sub-test scores; Untimed (30 minutes);
Equivalent Forms (2); Consumable; UK.

The *Edinburgh Reading Tests* were developed by
researchers commissioned by the Scottish Education
Department and the Educational Institute of Scotland.
The development work was guided by a steering
committee of teachers, psychologists and reading
specialists. The four stages of the Series cover the 7.00
to 16.00 age range and the tests are designed to
provide diagnostic information of help to the teacher
as well as giving a standardized measure of reading
attainment. The technical standard of the tests is very
high and although they were developed in Scotland
full norms are provided for England and Wales. A
more or less standard format was adopted for both the
development and presentation of the tests and they
have many general features in common. For example,
in content and organization the **Manual of Instructions** for each stage follows the same pattern and
some of the explanatory material is identical. Nevertheless, each test is designed as to be free-standing
and there are sufficient differences in detail to require
separate reviews of each test in the series. At the same
time, it will be clear that many of the general
comments made in this review of Stage 1 will apply to
succeeding stages.

Stage 1 differs from later stages in having two
parallel forms. These contain 91 items presented in
four sub-tests:

Vocabulary, (20 items). Word-to-picture matching
tasks and conventional sentence-completion are
used in this sub-test.

Syntax, (30 items). Three groups of items are
employed which deal with the child's knowledge of
structural aspects of sentences. The first ten items
consist of sentences which contain a superfluous
word which must be deleted to make the sentence
meaningful. A multiple-choice variant of cloze
procedure follows in which ten gaps in a prose
passage must be filled by selection of the appropriate words from sets of four. This is followed by a set
of ten single-sentence comprehension items designed to test the ability to understand spoken forms
of language presented in print. The Manual states
that while these tasks do not 'hang together in any
especially coherent way' they are all relevant to
making the transition from spoken to written language.

Sequences, (20 items). Items in this sub-test are
designed to check whether the child has a grasp of
'sequential factors necessary to his stage of development'. Firstly, a series of sentences with scrambled
word ordering are presented and the child must
identify the word which would start the sentence in
its unscrambled form. The last 11 items involve
matching short questions with their answers.

Comprehension, (21 items). The first two sets of
items are based on street-scene pictures. Answers to
the questions must be selected from notices, signs
and timetables which appear in the pictures. The
remaining items are based on four short passages in
which different attitudes and feelings are expressed
by four characters. The questions ask the child to
match the characters with particular views or
feelings.

Performance on the test may be recorded on the
profile sheet which is on the last page of the child's
test booklet. This contains space for a Quotient
(age-adjusted score). Standardized scores for each
sub-test may be represented graphically in four
separate bars or columns.

The 32-page Manual of Instructions is clear and
contains full sections on the statistical meaning of the
various test scores and step-by-step instructions for
drawing up individual profiles and identifying excep-
tionally high or low scores on each sub-test – a
convention followed in all stages in the series. There is
also a substantial discussion on the sub-tests and of
how the teacher might respond to the needs of
children with exceptional scores on particular sub-
tests.

Overall test reliability is high (KR20 = .94). Reliabilities for the four sub-tests range from .78 to .84. This is
slightly too low for any sub-test to be treated as a
reliable independent measure of ability in its own right.
The discussion of reliability does not distinguish

between forms of the test, nor is there evidence for inter-form correlation - an omission in an otherwise technically excellent test-development programme. Evidence for validity is based on endorsement of the steering committee for the development of the Edinburgh Series. Reference is made to experimental and correlational results to be published in a statistical annexe to the series. There is substantial intercorrelation between the four sub-tests – a general finding throughout the series. This would suggest that, whatever their apparent differences, they are probably measuring the same underlying process.

Standardization of the test was based on the scores of children aged 7.00 to 9.00 in a carefully selected representative sample of 2,500 Scottish children and 3,013 English and Welsh children in ordinary classes in state primary schools. Girls in the sample tended to do better than boys and Scottish children scored somewhat higher on average than those in the England and Wales sample. Regional and sex-based differences are found at all levels of the Edinburgh Series and these are generally in favour of girls and Scottish children. However, there are variations in the general pattern and it is important to check the precise nature of the differences for each test and to be sure that the most appropriate norms tables are employed. In the case of Stage 1 separate norms are given for

boys and girls and for both sexes combined, but not for the two regions. In later stages only regional differences are catered for in the main conversion tables. By careful inspection of the supplementary tables given in the manuals it would be possible to derive weighting factors which would take some account of additional differences in the sample, but this would also create obvious dangers of subsequent misunderstanding. Generally, it would not have detracted from the value of the tests if a single conversion table had been employed throughout and the regional and sex-based differences simply noted in supplementary tables.

The Edinburgh tests are distinguished by their relative length, as well as their technical standard. There is much to be said for tests which take a comprehensive and wide-ranging approach to reading although this can only be achieved at the expense of time and effort. Stage 1 certainly takes a broader approach to written language than other tests for the 7.00 plus age range. The model includes aspects of structure, organization and spoken usage which may well alert teachers to the need for worthwhile practical work. It would certainly be reasonable to argue that by 9.00 years of age a child should be able to successfully complete tasks of the sort used in Stage 1.

Edinburgh Reading Tests, Stage 2

**The Godfrey Thomson Unit,
University of Edinburgh**

1980 (Second Edition)

Hodder & Stoughton

Group; Objective; Standardized; 8.06–10.06; Reading Ages, Quotients (age-adjusted standardized scores), Standardized sub-test scores; Timed, 105 minutes over three sessions; Consumable; UK.

This second stage of the Edinburgh tests is administered in three sessions. In the first session a practice test is given which introduces the types of item used in Parts I and II of the main test.

Part I (second session)

Vocabulary, (20 items). A variety of procedures, including conventional sentence completion, are used to test knowledge of word meanings.

Comprehension of Sequence, (20 items). Six questions – asked by a policeman interrogating a witness – have to be matched with appropriate answers printed in scrambled order. A short account of the incident is then completed by selecting words to fill four gaps in a sentence. The final ten items involve re-ordering scrambled sentences.

Retention of Significant Details, (20 items). Two short passages must be read and factual recall of their content is tested by inserting words in sentence stems. This must be done without reference back to the stimulus passage.

Part II (third session)

Use of Context, (20 items). The sub-test begins with eight sentences in which one 'hard' word is underlined. A synonym for this word must be selected from a set of 12. The next eight items require selection of two-word synonyms. The last four items require selection of synonyms for 'clear', as it is used in four different sentences.

Reading Rate, (20 items). A standard speed of reading test format is employed in which pupils must read as much of a prose passage as possible in two minutes. There are 20 gaps in the passage where three alternative words are printed and the reader must choose the correct word to fill the gap.

Comprehension of Essential Ideas, (20 items). Sets of multiple-choice questions cover general and inferential aspects of comprehension of three prose passages.

The **Manual of Instructions** contains clear instructions for administering, marking and interpreting the test. The conversion tables for quotients, reading ages and sub-test scores closely follow the Stage 1 format. An overall internal consistency reliability – excluding Reading Rate – of .969 is quoted. Reliability for the sub-tests is fairly high, ranging from .814 to .913. Samples of 2,764 Scottish children and 2,745 English and Welsh children were used for standardization and details of age- and sex-based and regional differences in performance are tabulated. These show the general tendency for girls to perform somewhat better than boys. The general trend in the Edinburgh series is for performance of Scottish children to exceed that of the English and Welsh. However, in the Stage 2 standardization it was found that overall Scottish children did less well. No reasons are offered for this variation.

While the sub-tests in Stage 1 concentrated upon structural and organizational aspects of language, Stage 2 places greater emphasis upon comprehension processes. In principle this is sound. In practice some of the sub-tests employ somewhat more artificial or fragmented tasks than would be encountered in real-life reading. The Manual advises the teacher to check that low-scoring children have understood the instructions for sub-tests and this advice would be worth taking before attempting further interpretation. The subsequent advice on interpretation of sub-tests is generally clear, combining practical activities and general teaching strategies. However, it cannot be overlooked that the amount of work involved in administering, marking and then following up individual results would be considerable. It is reasonable to ask whether the quality of diagnostic information would justify the investment of time and effort. Reservations expressed over Stage 1 in this respect apply also to Stage 2 – perhaps with greater emphasis. Research into the measurement of comprehension skills by no means supports the general premise that comprehension is a multi-facet process composed of distinct sub-skills. On the other hand, it can be argued that certain distinctions can be useful for structuring and planning one's teaching – whatever the experimental evidence for their existence. Judged in this way, Stage 2 could perhaps be regarded as a thoughtful analysis of the problem.

Edinburgh Reading Tests, Stage 3

> **Moray House College of Education**
>
> **1981 (Second Edition)**
>
> **Hodder & Stoughton**

Group; Objective; Standardized; 10.00–12.06; Reading Ages, Quotients (age-adjusted standardized scores), Standardized sub-test scores; Timed, 110 minutes; Consumable; UK.

This third-stage test of the Edinburgh series consists of three parts. As in Stage 2 there is a practice test and Parts I and II of the test proper.

Part I

Reading for Facts, (35 items). Four short passages on factual topics are followed by lists of statements about the passages to be judged as 'True', 'False' or 'Doesn't Say'.

Comprehension of Sequences, (41 items). Nine short passages comprising four or five sentences are presented with the sentences in random order. The pupil must indicate the correct order for the sentences.

Retention of Main Ideas, (20 items). Multiple-choice questions dealing with main ideas or central facts in three passages have to be answered without reference back to the passages.

Part II

Comprehension of Points of View, (36 items). Four passages each present contrasting opinions of imaginary characters on certain topics. Each passage is followed by statements on the topic which must be attributed to the characters who would probably have made them.

Vocabulary, (35 items). A variety of formats, including sentence completion and synonym selection are used in this sub-test.

The general format of the **Manual of Instructions** closely follows that of Stage 2 and similar statistical details are presented. An overall internal-consistency reliability of .97 was found, with sub-test reliabilities ranging from .81 to .95. The principles of standardization closely follow Stages 1 and 2, involving two systematically selected samples of nearly 3,000 children. Full details of sex- and regionally-related differences in performance are given as in Stage 2, although the actual pattern of these differences is not identical.

There are both consistencies and contrasts in the models of reading adopted in Stages 2 and 3 of the series and it is worth asking how far the two tests represent a coherent developmental approach to reading in the middle years. Vocabulary and Comprehension of Sequences are retained in Stage 3, but Rate of Reading is 'dropped' and the Retention of Significant Details seems to have been replaced by Retention of Main Ideas. Use of Context is also discarded and Comprehension of Essential Ideas seems to have mutated into a Retention task. New to Stage 3 are Reading for Facts and Comprehension of Points of View. It can reasonably be argued that the latter process represents an increase in sophistication of reading skill but there is no discernible logic in any of the other changes in sub-test structure. Advice given on sub-test interpretation in either Manual is plausible taken in isolation but a cross-manual comparison reveals different interpretations of processes common to both tests. Certainly, there is no explanation of the relationship between the two stages.

It should be noted that the sub-tests in both stages tend to be substantially intercorrelated. The authors' claims that they are distinct is invalid by statistical criteria – most research into the nature of reading comprehension tends to show it is a unitary rather than multi-faceted skill. In this sense, therefore, the content-differences between the two stages are not so serious although Rate of Reading, as included in Stage 2, is probably a more psychologically discrete aspect of reading. This latter difference excepted, it could be said that both tests sample a wider 'universe' of reading comprehension skills of which the sub-tests are all closely related 'examples'. In effect, as global measures of reading attainment both tests are comparable in their validity.

Thus, if no diagnostic uses are proposed for the tests the problem of variation in content is of little importance. However, manuals of both tests discuss the diagnostic use of sub-test scores at some length and the teacher is encouraged to undertake what could well prove an extremely time-consuming exercise in following up individual performance. At this point it is important to know that the sub-tests upon which this process is to be based represent an optimal selection of reading competencies for the age group concerned. Herein lies a problem which has already been noted in the reviews of previous stages. The sub-tests may well guide the teacher towards activities of general educational value but there is no evidence that they were selected in preference to other possible sub-tests of *lesser* potential diagnostic value. Moreover, the unexplained differences between stages does nothing to

reassure the teacher that the necessary deliberations took place. In all, diagnostic teaching based on individual profiles should only be undertaken in a cautious and exploratory spirit. As the authors themselves point out, most children will perform at roughly the same level across sub-tests and it would be ill-advised to adopt any of the Edinburgh tests in the expectation that strikingly different profiles will be found across individual pupils or class groups.

Edinburgh Reading Tests, Stage 4

The Godfrey Thomson Unit,
University of Edinburgh

1977

Hodder & Stoughton

Group; Objective; Standardized; 12.00–16.00; Reading Ages, Quotients (age-adjusted standardized scores), Standardized sub-test scores; Timed, 60 minutes; Consumable; UK.

The final stage of the *Edinburgh Reading Tests* is in five sub-tests administered in two 30 minute sessions:

Skimming, (30 items). Three sets of ten questions must be answered rapidly by reference to three short texts. Pupils are instructed to read the questions first, then search the texts quickly to find single-word answers.

Vocabulary, (35 items). In all these items a synonym for a word in a sentence must be selected from five alternatives.

Reading for Facts, (30 items). Four passages are followed by sets of statements which must be rated as 'Agree', 'Disagree' or 'Doesn't Say' according to the content of the preceding passage.

Points of View, (35 items). Sets of statements on four topics must be matched to other statements with which they are consistent.

Comprehension, (25 items). This sub-test uses multiple-choice questions in the form of generally inferential statements about four prose passages.

The **Manual of Instructions** follows a similar format to manuals for preceding stages and provides a full and clear account of the interpretation of scores and the meaning of the sub-tests. Internal consistency reliability for the whole test is .956 and the sub-test reliabilities range from .732 to .911. As with other stages the sub-tests are intercorrelated and no evidence for validity against external criteria is presented. The standardization was carried out on 2,282 pupils in Scotland and 2,216 in England and Wales – difficulties in obtaining the original targets of 3,000 are reported. Overall girls performed slightly better than boys and a regional difference in favour of Scotland was found. While regionally-separate conversion tables are pro-vided there is also a rougher 'single-line' table based on the complete sample to allow comparison with norms for the whole sample.

The problem of discontinuity between stages is perhaps less acute than was the case with Stages 2 and 3. The Manual of Instructions notes that for secondary pupils it is preferable to think in terms of different reading 'tasks', rather than the 'skills' defined for earlier stages. It also refers to the problem of distinguishing between 'types of reading comprehension except in terms of a range of tasks which are commonly found'. It is worth wondering whether this focus upon task rather than skill might not have proved more profitable at earlier stages also.

Stage 4 of the *Edinburgh Reading Tests* is unquestionably the most suitable test currently available for assessing reading ability in the last two years of compulsory education. Its breadth and content would probably accord with many teachers' intuitions about the needs and interests of the age group. The reading material chosen emphasizes aspects of adult and working life, rather than the largely literary themes of the *NFER EH* series (q.v.). Although the material might not seem sufficiently intellectually testing for more able 15.00–16.00 year olds the conversion tables suggest that the test produces a reasonable spread of performance at this level. It is not possible to be quite so enthusiastic about its diagnostic potential. Here the reservations expressed over the earlier stages still apply.

GAP Reading Comprehension Test

J. McLeod
(UK edition prepared by Derick Unwin)

1970

Heinemann

Group; Objective; Standardized; 7.08–12.06; Reading Ages; Equivalent Forms (2); Consumable; Australia.

The GAP (named after a school in Australia) is a cloze comprehension test for 'regular' use in schools as a global measure of reading attainment.

Each form consists of seven or eight brief but unrelated passages from which approximately one word in ten has been deleted and a space of uniform length inserted. Alternatives to the specified correct word are not allowed in this test, although inaccurate spelling is not penalized. Scores are converted to reading ages and it is suggested that children take both Forms (B and R) and their total score aggregated to give a more accurate result. A correlation of .83 between the two forms is given as the basis of test-retest reliability but the details of this are not quite clear – the **Manual** claims that combining the forms represents an 88-item test of .91 reliability, yet each form contains only 42 items. The Manual describes how the development of the GAP entailed validation exercises involving correlations with other tests. These include a correlation of .73 with *Schonell Silent Reading Test B* on the British standardization sample. The original standardization of the GAP was carried out with over 2,000 Australian children in about 1965 and an additional standardization was carried out some time later with over 1,000 children in Aberdeen, Glamorgan, London and Suffolk. This probably constitutes a reasonable cross-section for the British norms.

The test is simple to administer and seems to enjoy some popularity amongst British teachers. There is certainly plenty of general evidence for the validity of cloze procedure as a measure of reading comprehension and the GAP has performed effectively in a number of research studies. As a free-standing cloze comprehension test the GAP is probably the equal of any other published tests available for the age range although the brevity of the passages, the absence of standardized scores and the absence of a full-scale UK standardization make it less than ideal.

GAPADOL Reading Comprehension

J. McLeod and J. Anderson

1973

Heinemann

Group; Objective; Standardized; 7.03–16.11; Reading Ages; Timed, 30 minutes; Equivalent Forms (2); Consumable; Australia.

GAPADOL is designed to measure levels of reading ability in the secondary age range. A special score table makes identification of retarded and superior readers particularly convenient. The test is intended as an extension to the GAP which the authors consider to have an 'effective ceiling at reading age 10' and accurate in discriminating retardation only in children less than 12 years – a point not mentioned in the GAP Manual.

As with the GAP there are two equivalent forms (Y and G) containing a series of paragraphs with approximately every tenth word deleted. These are printed in two unusually elongated **test booklets.** As a consequence the test passages are printed in long columns consisting of lines of only five or six words. There are two practice passages and six test passages. The pupil must write the missing words in boxes on the adjacent page, alongside the deletions. The length of missing words is indicated by the number of dashes in the blank space. Only the marking-key-specified word is marked correct. It is recommended that both forms of the test are applied and an aggregate score used to increase reliability and sensitivity of the test. Internal consistency reliability coefficients are presented for five different year groups, with a median, or middle point, value of .91. No information is provided about the standardization (is it possible the publishers have assumed the original Australian norms are satisfactory?) nor is any specific validity evidence presented.

There are few standardized reading attainment tests for the secondary age range and this test would provide a quick general guide to reading ability at this level. However, it ignores the variety and specialization of written material in secondary education. This problem is more effectively tackled in *Edinburgh Reading Test Stage 4* (q.v.) which also appears to discriminate more effectively between reading ages between 15.00 and 16.00. The GAPADOL continues with reading ages up to 16.11 but little reliance can be attached to these as the increase in scores with age is slight. This probably reflects the absence of any real difference in reading skill between age groups above 16.00 years in the general population of the UK.

Gates-Macginitie Reading Tests, Levels R, A, B, C, D, E, F (Second Edition)

W. H. Macginitie

1978

NFER-NELSON

Group; Objective; Standardized (for US pupils only); 6.06–17.00+; Various Standardized Scales; Timed, 55–65 minutes (two sessions); Equivalent Forms (2–3); Consumable (but separate answer sheets levels D, E and F); US.

The *Gates-Macginitie Reading Tests* are a series of American tests, first published in 1965 and produced as a re-standardized second edition in 1978. The current series make it possible to monitor and record progress throughout primary and secondary education using successive levels of the tests. However, none of the tests are standardized for British populations and many teachers will have misgivings about the appropriateness of the available American norms. Nevertheless, it is worth noting that when Level A of the previous edition of the test was standardized with British children the relationship between average scores for children of different age or grade levels in the two countries was very close.

By converting the US grade levels to chronological age groups the UK distributors of the tests suggest the following age groups for the tests:

Level	Age Range
R	5 – 7
A	5 – 7
B	7 – 8
C	8 – 9
D	9 – 12
E	13 – 16
F	16 – 18

The above ages are no more than an approximate guide to suitability and closer examination of the materials would be essential before electing to use any particular test on a large scale.

All levels except R are divided into two main sections, Vocabulary and Comprehension, containing over 40 items each. Levels A and B use a simple multiple-choice picture-selection technique. In the Vocabulary items one of four words must be chosen to match a target picture and in the Comprehension part one of four pictures must be chosen to match a short statement or answer a direct question. In subsequent levels Vocabulary is tested by multiple-choice synonym matching and Comprehension by a series of prose passages followed by two or more multiple-choice questions. Inevitably some of the material reflects the interest, experience and cultural background of American children, although much of the pictorial material and language would be within the grasp of British children. In Level R there are four sub-sets of items testing letter sounds, vocabulary, letter recognition and comprehension. Picture identification tasks are used for most of the items.

A general impression of the quality of the series can be gained by considering the Level A Test. This consists of 45 vocabulary items and 40 comprehension items. These are contained in a 12-page **test booklet**, the back page being used for practice before commencing the main tests. The tests are given in two sessions and the author suggests that 20 minutes are needed for preparing the pupil for the vocabulary test and 15 minutes for the comprehension test. Machine-scorable versions of the test booklets are available to users in America and advice is given for using these.

Performance is recorded on the cover of the test booklet. Scores may be expressed in a number of forms (stanines, normal curve equivalents, percentile ranks, grade equivalents and extended scale scores). These may be transferred to a **Class Summary Record.** A **Decoding Skills Analysis Form** provides a way of putting to additional practical use the time spent on the test, by organizing the errors that individual pupils have made. Readers' errors thus yield possible clues to what they still need to be taught. There might be some scope for this diagnostic application of the test with British children, as the procedure is not dependent upon normative considerations. Level B has a similar diagnostic facility and with Level R a sub-test profile can be constructed.

However, tests for the older age groups incorporate few diagnostic functions.

The **Teachers' Manual** is full and clearly written, although it is a little daunting at first sight and some of the matters discussed are not relevant to education in the UK. Information is given about the reliability and validity of all tests in the series. Internal consistency reliability ranges from .90 to .95 for Vocabulary and .88 to .94 for Comprehension and guidelines are given for determining test validity in relation to curricula in one's own school. The standard of design and presentation is high throughout.

Although the *Gates-Macginitie Reading Tests* have a number of attractive features – including the luxury of computerized marking – they cannot be seriously recommended for use in Britain without the necessary anglicization and British standardization. Furthermore, they are somewhat limited in the scope of skills tested and it cannot be said they embody a model of reading dramatically superior to those of indigenous tests.

Group Literacy Assessment

Frank A. Spooncer

1982

Hodder & Stoughton

Group; Objective; Standardized; 7.04–14.00; Standardized Scores, Reading Ages; Timed, 16 minutes; Consumable; UK.

The *Group Literacy Assessment* gives a single measure of attainment based on a composite task of reading and spelling. A number of practical uses are specified; all centre on problems of screening and surveying in the final primary or first secondary year.

The Test is printed on a **single sheet.** Side one contains a short prose passage, headed with an illustration. Thirty-six of the words in the passage are misspelled and one mark is awarded for each one identified. A second mark is given if the child can provide the correct spelling. Side two contains a 32-item cloze test in which initial letters of missing words are given, and their exact length is indicated by broken lines. Two marks are awarded for correct spelling of the missing word. No credit is given otherwise.

The 14-page **Manual** gives the necessary administration and marking instructions and a standardized score conversion table for the 10.06 to 12.06 age range. There is also a Reading Age scale from 7.04 to 14.00 years. A particularly clear discussion of the relative meaning and merits of the two forms of scoring is included. A further system of 'Literacy Categories' on an A to D scale is suggested, based on raw scores. There is some comment on the nature and problems of 'C' and 'D' children, although this centres on reading rather than spelling.

An internal consistency reliability of .95 is cited, although it is noted this may be a slightly 'inflated' estimate. There is evidence of correlations with a number of other published tests. For example, correlations of .81 and .78 with Test 12 of Daniels and Diack's *Standard Reading Tests* (q.v.) were found for boys and girls respectively in a group of 2,544 first-year secondary children in the standardization sample.

The full standardization sample appears to have been larger than this. including 2,488 junior leavers and 1,886 third-year pupils in junior high schools in the London Borough of Waltham Forest. However, the latter group does not seem to have been used to obtain the standardized score tables. The reading ages were derived from 'calibration' with Daniels and Diack Test 12 and the *Group Reading Assessment* (q.v.). Purists might question the value of this 'cut-price' strategy particularly given the questionable status of Daniels and Diack's norms.

The test is inexpensive, has recent norms and is designed to appeal to children. Nevertheless, there is a fundamental ambiguity in the way spelling and reading are combined. There seems to be no real advantage in such a compound measure. Spelling and reading ability are not necessarily related (some good readers are poor spellers) and psychologically the two processes are quite distinct. The test is perhaps best regarded as a 'reading dependent test of spelling'.

Group Reading Assessment

Frank A. Spooncer

1964

Hodder & Stoughton

Group; Objective; Standardized; 7.08–9.00; Reading Ages, Quotients (standardized scores); Timed, 30 minutes; Consumable; UK.

The *Group Reading Assessment* was designed for the particular purpose of assessing objectively the reading level of children at the end of their first year in a junior school.

The four-page **test booklet** contains 57 items which are presented in three parts:

Part One, (16 items). The child has to find, in a group of five words, the one spoken by the teacher. To avoid any ambiguity the teacher includes the required word in a simple sentence.

Part Two, (25 items). From a group of four words, one has to be selected which the child thinks best fits into a printed sentence.

Part Three, (16 items). After reading for them-selves the first word in a line, children must find other words in that line which are pronounced in exactly the same way. Two words have to be found in some lines, ensuring that all the words are read; this considerably reduces the chances of success by guessing.

Performance on the test is recorded on the front page of the pupil's booklet. The latter contains spaces for recording the scores for each part of the test, and for the child's reading age.

The 16-page **Manual of Instructions** gives clear directions for the administration and scoring of the test, as well as the procedure for converting raw scores to reading ages and standardized scores. The rationale for the content of the test is clearly set out; this was determined after discussions with teachers as to which aspects of reading they attached most importance. In order to represent 'two schools of thought', both the mechanical and comprehension aspects of reading were included.

The main standardization was based on a sample of 2,200 children aged 7.08–9.00 in one London borough. Supporting evidence was obtained from the administration of the test in other parts of the country and from scores for over 8,000 children in a separate London borough. Overall test reliability is high (KR20 = .97). Validity was established by comparing raw scores for groups of children with their reading ages on other published reading tests. Although the harder items may demand a skill in comprehension, the aim of the test is largely designed to test mechanical reading. The validity data confirm that the main aim has been achieved.

The test has been widely used since its publication in 1964; the ninth impression being dated 1979. Class teachers should note the original purpose of the test – that of surveying the reading levels of complete age groups of children at the end of their first year in a junior school. It is not suitable for infants and is not recommended for use in the first term of the junior school. It can be helpful as a means of grouping children quickly and conveniently by reading ability, and used judiciously, the test may provide a quick method of finding the most backward readers on entry to secondary school. It must be stressed however, that reading ages can only be obtained in the range 6.04 – 11.08 and that the standardization applies to first-year juniors.

Users of the test have found that it is suitable for the specific age groups described in the Manual. Although the test is easy to administer, there will inevitably be some less able readers who will need additional help in following the directions.

Group Reading Test (Second Edition)

D. Young

1980

Hodder & Stoughton

Group; Objective; Standardized; 6.05–12.10; Reading Ages, Quotients (standardized scores); Timed, 13 minutes; Equivalent forms (2); Consumable; UK.

This second edition of the widely-used *Group Reading Test* has up-dated norms. However, the content of the test remains unchanged. The test has proved particularly popular with LEAs as a large-scale screening and monitoring device.

Each form of the test is comprised of 45 items printed on a single **test sheet:**

  Side One, (15 items). One of between three to five words must be selected to match a picture.

  Side Two, (30 items). The child is required to select suitable definitions from six words presented in multiple-choice sentence-completion format.

Special **templates** are provided to facilitate marking and performance on the test is recorded on the front page of the pupil's test sheet. Provision is made for entering the raw score and the reading quotient. The **Manual** provides conversion tables for converting raw scores to reading quotients for the age range 6.05–12.10 and reading ages range 5.04–10.00 years.

The test was designed for use with children in the final year (especially in the last term) of the infants' stage and in the first year (especially in the first term) of the junior stage, and with older, below-average pupils. The layout of the test was partly influenced by the decision to use a template for ease of scoring.

The new norms are based on surveys carried out between 1974 and 1979 in three separate areas. These involved some 21,711 infants, 5,560 first-year juniors and 1,876 pupils ages 8.07 – 12.00. Variations from the original norms are ascribed to the distortions produced by combining the score distribution of several groups to construct a single common table. Details on the standardization and reliability of the test related to the latest norms should suffice to answer critics of the earlier standardization procedures. The

Manual records some particularly thorough reliability studies and tabulates in some detail data concerning differences between scores on re-testing. Generally, these indicate sound test reliability; a correlation of .945 between the two forms is cited. Correlations between the *Group Reading Test* and tests such as the *Neale Analysis of Reading Ability* (q.v.), *Vernon's Graded Word Reading Test* and *NFER Reading Test AD* (q.v.) generally exceed .87 – indicating a substantial 'concurrent' validity.

The Manual states that the test may be suitable for older, below-average pupils. However, it must be remembered that its main purpose is for children in their last year of the infant school and in their first year of the junior school. A weakness of the test, therefore, may be the attempt to cover too wide an age range with a relatively small number of items.

Poor readers may find side two of the test difficult and need reassurance that the task required of them is the same as that demonstrated with the sample items on side one. In order to present the test on one sheet of the paper, there is inevitably a 'crowding' of items which may even present some confusion to readers of average ability.

The Young test is economical in time and money and this may explain why it is now widely used in many schools and local authorities for the purpose of screening the seven-plus age group. It is for this reason that a fresh look at the design of the Manual and the pupil's test sheet would be valuable.

Holborn Reading Scale

A.F. Watts

1948

Harrap (distributed by the Test Agency)

Individual; Objective; Standardized; 5.09–13.09; Reading Ages; Untimed; Re-usable; UK.

The test consists of thirty-three sentences arranged in order of difficulty, both as regards their mechanical elements and comprehensibility. The sentences are printed on a single sheet from which the child must read. The child is asked to see how many of the sentences can be read, the teacher being permitted to tell him the words he is unable to name until altogether he has failed to name four. Figures opposite the sentence in which he has registered his fourth failure indicate the child's reading age. There is a three-month difference between each sentence read. The **Manual** includes a list of questions relating to each test sentence and the author suggests that a comparison can be made between a child's mechanical reading and comprehension. There is little information on reliability and validity of the test.

The Holborn achieved popularity mainly because of its ease and speed of individual administration and the simple way to obtain a reading age. It was welcomed by many teachers as an alternative to the word recognition tests which required the pupil to read words in isolation.

Despite withdrawal of the test at one time by the publishers, teachers continued to use it, often without reference to the Manual. In one county the test was still being widely used in 1982, the form from which the pupil was asked to read often being in a dilapidated state.

Given the archaic language of the test and the inadequate process of standardization, it was surprising to find that it was reissued in 1980 and further reprinted in 1980 and 1982. The reprinting would appear to reflect the demand for the test by many teachers. Bookbinder has more recently published the *Salford Sentence Reading Test* (q.v.) which is similar to the word recognition part of the Holborn Scale with the added advantage of three parallel forms of the test.

Teachers often claim that they find the Holborn a useful means of monitoring children's reading progress. This is surprising when the test and the manual are so clearly out of date. Doubts must be also expressed on the validity of requiring children to read single, unconnected sentences out of context.

Hunter-Grundin Literacy Profiles, Level One to Level Four

Elizabeth Hunter-Grundin and Hans Grundin

1980

The Test Agency

Group with Individual sections; Objective and Judgemental sections; Standardized (reading and spelling); 6.04–8.05 (Level One), 7.10–9.03 (Level Two), 8.10–10.03 (Level Three), 10.00+ (Level Four); Reading Ages, Standardized Scores, A to E Grades (Spoken and Written Language); Timed, 30 minutes (group sections) plus 3-5 minutes per child; Consumable; UK.

The Literacy Profiles give normative and qualitative measures of four (or five) aspects of spoken and written language. They are specifically designed for monitoring and recording progress during the primary years. The authors also stress the importance of linking testing with 'diagnostic teaching'.

The four levels follow a similar general format:

Reading for Meaning (45 to 60 items). A modified multiple-choice version of cloze procedure. Missing words in a continuous prose passage are supplied by selecting from sets of four given alternatives.

Spelling (20 to 25 items). An orally administered test in which target words are presented in the course of a narrative passage read aloud by the teacher. Children follow the narrative in their test paper and write the target words in the corresponding spaces.

Free Writing. Children are instructed to write for ten minutes on 'On the Way to School'. Efforts are assessed on the 'basis of expert judgement' according to A to E scales for Legibility, Fluency, Accuracy and Originality. Guidance is given in the form of both explanation and examples of written work.

Spoken Language. An individual test in which the child is encouraged to describe what is going on in a stimulus picture. Rating scales A to E are used for Confidence, Enunciation, Vocabulary, Accuracy and Imagination.

Attitudes to Reading (Levels One and Two only). Children indicate their liking for reading as an activity, relative to five other activities, by choosing one of five 'funny faces'. These represent a scale of liking reflected in the expression of each face, ranging from a scowl ('dislike very much') to a broad smile ('like very much'). A similar format is used to let children indicate briefly how much they liked doing the Reading and Spelling tests.

A **checklist** is included for recording judgements of spoken and written performance. This may be kept, together with other completed test booklets in a cumulative **Record Wallet.** The Wallet's cover bears a printed form for recording performance on successive levels of the Profiles

Separate **Reference Books** (manuals) accompany each level. This is perhaps an unnecessary duplication of material. The Books are fairly long, running to over 40 pages, and contain similar detailed guidance on administration and interpretation, together with practical advice on follow-up teaching. An adequate account of the standardization procedures is given, together with supplementary information on socio-economic variations behind the norms. The numbers of children used in standardization are not as large as those used in certain other tests, particularly NFER-produced ones, nor is it clear how far the schools involved were selected according to principles of representative sampling. Nevertheless, the norms obtained are probably satisfactory as a general yardstick for measuring progress. No real 'norms' are provided for the spoken and free writing tasks although the authors imply a normative status for the grading system. For example, an E grade represents the 'overall free writing ability of the lowest 5–10 per cent'. This assumes, amongst other things, that an individual teacher's judgement will accord precisely with that of the test authors. It should be noted that the reading age tables for each level give a wider range of age-equivalents than is possible with the standardized scores. For example, Level One gives reading ages from 6.00 to 9.00 and Level Two 6.00 to 10.09. Internal consistency reliability coefficients for the Reading and Spelling tasks are generally high, in the range .90 to .98, but no reliability evidence is offered for the other tests. It is wisely suggested that teachers should practise and confer when using the judgemental sections to maximize the consistency and agreement of their judgements. Exercises of this sort would seem essential if the Profiles are to be used formally for recording progress. Validity for the Reading for Meaning test is shown through substantial correlations with other tests although no details of the number of children involved are given. Irritatingly, there is recurring reference to 'construct validity' when it is evident that it is really 'face validity' – the extent to which a test *appears* to measure whatever it claims to measure – that is intended.

The Profiles can be criticized as time-consuming to score and interpret, although not to administer. However, they are comprehensive by intention and thoughtful and systematic assessment cannot be made without a time investment. It can also be argued that

some of the processes graded in spoken and written work are not strictly linguistic. This would be to miss the point of their central educational importance.

Overall, the *Hunter-Grundin Literacy Profiles* are a dramatic improvement over most previously published methods of testing language in primary education. They meet an acute need for a system of assessment which is cumulative and comprehensive. The tests appear to have been developed with great care for both their practicality and appeal and they deserve serious consideration as possible keystones in language monitoring in schools. Sadly, some schools may be tempted to use only the reading and spelling materials because of their ease of scoring and stronger normative basis.

London Reading Test

ILEA Research and Statistics Group

1978

NFER-NELSON

Group; Mainly Objective; Standardized; 10.07–12.04; Standardized Scores; Untimed (60 minutes); Equivalent Forms (2); Consumable; UK.

The main purpose of this test is for use as a survey/screening test to be used at time of transfer from primary to secondary school. It aims to demonstrate the child's ability to comprehend a written passage. This information forms the basis on which selection of children for remedial teaching is made. It was designed originally for use in Inner London schools but has been nationally standardized and the content would be relevant in many urban and multi-cultural settings.

Test A and the equivalent Test B each consist of three passages designed to be culturally relevant to ILEA children and linked to the level of difficulty of the textbooks used in the first year in ILEA secondary schools. The first and second sections are cloze procedure passages whilst the third is continuous prose followed by questions designed to assess the more able reader's higher order comprehension skills, including inferential comprehension and evaluative response to 'open' questions. Specific reference was made to Barrett's 'taxonomy' of reading comprehension in preparing questions for the third test passage. This is a useful starting point for thinking about the teaching and assessment of reading comprehension although Barrett's taxonomy is sometimes regarded with greater reverence than is appropriate. As the Manual notes, 'it is only one of the possible hierarchies of comprehension skills'.

The **test booklets** are attractively presented and include two full-page illustrations. There is a separate teaching passage which must be completed and discussed before the test is taken, and a **Teacher's Manual** which gives a clear explanation of the theoretical basis of the test, as well as marking keys and administration instructions. The Manual states that the internal-consistency reliability is .95 for ILEA, and .93 nationally. Validity correlation coefficients of .80 and above are given for a number of well-established oral reading tests. Separate ILEA and national norms are provided at both junior (10.07–12.01) and secondary level (10.11–12.04). The national norms are based on the performance of 10,000 children who took Form A and sub-samples of 1,000 who took Form B. The ILEA norms are somewhat more lenient than the national norms although the former would perhaps be informative when assessing children in other urban multi-cultural settings. The secondary norms are also generally more lenient than those for juniors. A score of 44 on Form A earns a standardized score of 100 for a junior 11.00-year-old and 102 for a secondary 11.00-year-old. This reflects a deterioration in academic performance over the summer break which few other standardized tests take account of. However, the test was designed for use with fourth-year juniors and the secondary norms are perhaps of ancillary interest. If the results are to be used for screening, placement or grouping on transfer to secondary school, it is essential that the test should be given in the non-threatening surroundings of the primary school during the child's final term. This avoids the necessity for testing, and its attendant anxiety, within the first days of the child's secondary school career.

The *London Reading Test* is an excellent example of a test which has been developed with both a specific purpose and target group of readers in mind. It also breaks new ground in standardized reading testing by using open and evaluative questioning. How effectively it indicates a child's capacity to meet the reading demands of early secondary work has yet to be formally examined. Certainly, for it to be used effectively on transfer, liaison and cooperation between primary and secondary schools would be essential. For example, it would be important that the test was administered and scored in sufficient time for the results to be useful to the secondary school.

Neale Analysis of Reading Ability

Marie D. Neale
1966 (Second Edition)
Macmillan Education

Individual; Partly Objective; Standardized; 7.00–11.00; Reading Ages; Untimed; Equivalent Forms (3); Consumable Record Sheets; UK.

The Neale was first published in 1958 to be used by classroom teachers, as well as in clinical settings, for qualitative assessment of individual reading difficulties based largely on oral reading performance. Inspection of the *Durrell Analysis of Reading Difficulty* (q.v) suggests that this test provided the model and pattern for the Neale. In practice the Neale is widely used to assess reading attainment and it is therefore reviewed in this section, rather than alongside other diagnostic tests.

Each of the three equivalent forms (A, B and C) of the test contains six short stories of increasing length and complexity. These are printed on semi-stiff pages of a **ring-bound booklet**. The following skills are tested:

Main Test: Reading Accuracy (number of oral errors)
Comprehension
Speed of Reading
Supplementary Diagnostic Tests:
Names and Sounds of Letters
Auditory Discrimination
Syllable Blending and Recognition

The Reading Accuracy test is scored by recording the number of errors the child makes in reading each passage. A separate individual **Record Sheet** is used to record these and categorize them as 'mispronunciations', 'substitutions', 'refusals', 'omissions' and 'reversals'. Repetitions are noted but not categorized. Comprehension is based on questions requiring recall of simple information in the passages and a record is made of the time taken to complete each passage. It seems possible this measure of Speed of Reading is not always used in practice.

The 37-page **Manual** describes the rationale for the development of the test and gives administration instructions for the three main test measures. Reliability and validity are based on relatively small numbers of children and the validity coeffients, although high, are based on studies with obsolete tests. Standardization was carried out using 2000 children in the 7.00 to 11.00 age range in 13 schools. Relatively small numbers were used for standardization of forms B and C and separate reading age tables are not used for different forms. It must be assumed that materials in the three forms were sufficently closely matched in difficulty to render separate tables superfluous.

The three additional diagnostic tests are printed in the reading test booklet but the instructions for their use and interpretation are somewhat general and tentative. It may be useful to have letter-recognition and blending tests available in such a printed form but the value of the Auditory test, which uses a simple spelling task, is less clear.

The Neale Analysis is certainly widely used, and respected, by teachers, remedial specialists and psychologists. However, it is now outmoded in some crucial respects. The standardization is too dated to justify the continued use of the test as a normative measure. The content is also in dire need of modernization: one of the stories deals with a 'milkman's horse wandering in the fog' and the illustrations are redolent of the mid-1950s. The language in the final passages can also be criticized as unnecessarily tortuous by modern standards ('In reproof, the subterranean cauldron suddenly exploded violently'). The system of error analysis also deserves reappraisal. Work by the Goodmans and Marie Clay has shown that there are many more fruitful categories of oral reading behaviour than those applied in the Neale, indeed more knowledgeable users of the test already take account of such developments.

The Neale offers a general format and approach which has time-proven value to the teacher. It is to be hoped that this may encourage the publishers to consider the production of a much-needed successor.

NFER Reading Test A

National Foundation for Educational Research

1972

NFER-NELSON

Group; Objective; Standardized; 6.09–8.09; Standardized Scores; Untimed (20–30 minutes); Consumable; UK.

This test consists of 38 sentence-completion type items preceded by four practice items. It is designed to test reading comprehension in the first year of the junior school.

Performance on the test is recorded on the front page of the eight-page test booklet. Standardized scores are recorded, not reading ages.

The eight-page **Manual** gives directions for administering and scoring the test. The method of standardization based on sampling in five different areas is discussed and the difference in scores between boys and girls at the first year junior stage is reported.

The earlier manual included a correction formula to take account of guessing, which can influence scores on some multiple-choice tests. However, a study completed in 1972 showed that there were no significant differences in the rank order between corrected and uncorrected scores adjusted for age allowance. The KR20 reliability of the test is given as 0.96.

Reading Test A has been widely used in Britain. It has been found to be of special value for assessing reading comprehension of children in the first year of the junior school. Some children may come outside the norms for the test and for these, individual testing on other tests may be desirable. The merit in the provision of standardized scores in preference to reading ages is now more widely accepted but some class teachers may still be disappointed that the latter are not readily accessible in this test.

NFER Reading Test AD

A.G. Watts

1978 (standardization)

NFER-NELSON

Group; Objective; Standardized; 8.00–10.07; Standardized Scores; Timed, 15 minutes; Consumable; UK.

No specific guidance is given concerning the purpose of Test AD. It is generally used for obtaining a global measure of reading attainment for screening, grouping and monitoring.

The test consists of 35 sentence stems. One of five alternative final words must be selected to meaningfully complete the sentence. This technique of 'sentence-completion' is widely used in published reading tests. The **Manual** contains information on administering and marking the test together with standardized score conversion tables and an account of the most recent 1977 standardization survey. This test has a long history and the language of some test items has been slightly modernized. Comparison of the 1977 norms, based on over 9,000 children, with those previously published (1955, 1966) shows the test may prove slightly easier for today's children. Internal consistency reliability coefficients of .92 are quoted and the Manual explains how this relates to the standard error of the test. Interestingly, somewhat higher test-retest values (.91–.97) were given in previous versions of the Manual. These are not mentioned, although, perhaps unnecessarily, a detailed discussion of guessing effects is retained. No evidence for validity is given.

Reading Test AD has been widely used in primary schools and its sales must surely run into millions. It can be regarded as the definitive sentence-completion test and the review comments which follow apply equally to other sentence-completion tests reviewed in this volume.

Sentence-completion tests measure many of the skills in reading: decoding and word recognition; memory span; linguistic knowlege (particularly syntactic); reading experience; social and cultural knowledge; vocabulary; limited use of context. Also, such tests correlate highly with other forms of reading test and with teacher's rankings of children's reading ability. They also tend to be statistically highly reliable and can conveniently be constructed to cover wide ability and age ranges by suitable grading of items. They are quickly administered and marked and tend to be cheap to produce. Schools and LEAs have found them useful in large-scale screening and monitoring. Prior to the establishment of the APU they were used to monitor national reading standards amongst 11- and 15-year-olds.

In spite of this widespread acceptance sentence-completion tests are often criticized by reading specialists. The central objection concerns the artificality of sentence completion and its lack of relation to either theories of reading or defensible teaching aims or curricula. Where, other than in a sentence-completion test is a reader confronted with a list of entirely unrelated sentences with words missing from them? Reading, even in the early stage, involves working with more or less connected prose and the purposes to which reading may be put are diverse. Neither of these major considerations is reflected by sentence completion. In effect sentence completion bears little relation to real-life reading or to teaching methods. If we accept that our methods of assessment should reflect the aims and methods of teaching the role for sentence-completion tests will be limited. Sadly, the tests which more faithfully follow tenable models of good practice tend to be less economical in every respect and, by default, the sentence-completion test has lingered on.

NFER Reading Test BD

NFER Guidance and Assessment Service

1971

NFER-NELSON

Group; Objective; Standardized; 7.00–10.04 (Provisional Norms 10.00–11.04); Standardized Scores; Timed, 20 minutes; Consumable; UK.

Reading Test BD is similar to *Reading Test AD* (q.v.) in purpose and content, but BD has 44 items. The Manuals are also similar in format but the BD **Manual** also contains some details concerning studies of guessing although, paradoxically, a different conclusion is reached – possibly as a result of slight differences in methods of investigation. Both Manuals contain results of a comparative study of AD and BD. This suggests that although BD's standardization dates from a 1969 survey with large samples of children in Oxfordshire, Portsmouth, Preston and Surrey, the standards set by the 1969 conversion tables are still appropriate.

Internal consistency reliability is high (.9495) and in previous editions of the Manual test-retest values of .90 to .92 were quoted. No validity data are presented, although reference is made to a study of correlations with teachers' estimates of reading ability.

Reading Test BD is standardized for a wider age range than Test AD, although norms for 10.00 to 11.04 are provisional. It is certainly, in raw score terms, a slightly harder test. Items in BD tend to be longer, if not more verbose. Both tests suffer from the unfortunate inanity which arises from writing, not to interest or inform one's readers, but merely to test their reading ability. Item 35 of BD observes 'the probability that you would succeed in an attempt to swim the Atlantic is zero because failure would be absolutely (certain)', while Item 20 of AD proclaims that 'The nation expects both adults and children to look right and left in crossing (thoroughfares)'.

NFER Reading Tests EH1, 2, 3

S.M. Bate

1975

NFER-NELSON

Group; Objective; Standardized; 11.00–15.11; Standardized Scores; Timed, 25 minutes (EH1), 45 minutes (EH2), 4–2 minutes (EH3); Consumable; UK.

The EH series can be treated as a battery of three separate tests providing general measures of reading attainment. The tests are suitable for screening, monitoring and survey exercises in the secondary age range.

EH1 is a sentence-completion test of reading vocabulary containing 60 items. EH2 is a comprehension test, mainly multiple-choice, based on seven passages each followed by five items involving both inferential and contextual skills as well as knowledge of word meanings. EH3 is a strictly-timed rate of reading test in which pupils must read two continuous prose passages. Progress is indicated by responding to simple sentence-completion items embedded in the passage.

EH1 and 2 share a single **Manual** which seems to have borrowed, somewhat unconvincingly, ideas from *NFER Reading Comprehension Test DE* (q.v.) Manual for the introductory remarks. The description of the standardization of the two tests reveals that while a total of over 17,000 pupils were involved they were drawn from five LEAs and tested on different occasions between 1971 to 1974. The resulting norms, although quite adequate for practical purposes, are thus something of a conglomeration. Only a typewritten **Manual** is provided for EH3 – suggesting a limited demand for the test. The Manual itself implies that both norms and marking procedures are still provisional, although the test has been in print for many years. The standardization tables for all three tests include the usual age adjustment; however, inspection reveals that the tendency for raw score to increase with chronological age is relatively mild.

No evidence for test validity is presented, but internal consistency reliabilities for EH1 range from .90 to .94 and for EH2 from .81 to .88.

The EH 1-3 series does have an advantage in standardization for a fuller secondary age range than most other reading tests. The series also provides, at face value, separate measures in three areas and thus has a slight advantage of breadth, although, in practice, all three tests are not always used in combination and no advice on their use to produce diagnostic profiles is given.

The inclusion of a test of rate of reading is an implicit acknowledgement of the diverse nature of mature reading, but it is a far from adequate one. Apart from these slight advantages the EH series has little to recommend it. Younger secondary pupils will find the tests difficult while the essentially literary tone of the tests makes them less than ideal for assessing the more backward older pupils. The circumstances in which it is necessary to assess reading of pupils above the age of 13.00 may be limited and specialized, nevertheless there is an urgent need to produce more suitable means for doing so than those provided by EH1-3.

NFER Reading Tests SR-A and SR-B

NFER Guidance and Assessment Service

1979

NFER-NELSON

Group; Objective; Standardized; 7.06–11.11; Standardized Scores; Timed, 20 minutes; Equivalent Forms (2); Consumable; UK.

SR-A and SR-B are equivalent versions of a 48-item sentence-completion test. In the past supply of this test was restricted to LEA representatives such as advisers and psychologists who wished to carry out official screening and survey programmes using test items pupils will not have encountered in school. However, the tests are now supplied directly to schools. Some items in SR-A/B are in fact taken from other closed NFER tests, such as NS6 – a test used in many national surveys of reading attainment.

The **Manual** describes the 1978 standardization of SR-A on a sample of 13,868 children, and the calibration of SR-B on over 3,000 children who took both tests. Although this appears to be a 'short-cut' method of devising standardization tables the results are only marginally less authoritative than those for SR-A. In fact, while separate tables are given for each version they give a very similar pattern of score conversion, as would be expected from such closely matched tests.

Internal consistency reliability ranges from .85 to .87. Strangely, no result is given for the inter-correlation of the two forms, although this would probably be high. No validity data are provided, although the manual notes that sentence completion correlates highly with other measures of reading.

In the past, this pair of tests has proved useful to LEAs engaged in screening and monitoring complete age-group populations where cost, time and convenience are of paramount importance. Nevertheless, there are dangers in the continued use of such an insensitive index of reading attainments during a period of severe contraction in LEA expenditure. The subtler early signs of deterioration would certainly not be detected by such tests.

Primary Reading Test Levels 1 and 2 (Revised Edition)

Norman France

1981

NFER-NELSON

Group; Objective; Standardized; 6.00–12.00; Reading Ages; Standard Age Scores, Stanines, Percentiles; Untimed (30 minutes); Equivalent Forms (2); Consumable; UK (separate norms for Scotland).

The *Primary Reading Test* is a general test of reading attainment suitable for screening, monitoring and grouping purposes. Provision of both two levels and two forms particularly aids long-term progress testing.

Level 1 (6.00–10.00) contains 16 word-picture matching tasks and 32 sentence-completion tasks. This level can be administered as an individual test of word recognition as well as in group form. Separate norms are provided for this easier mode of testing. Level 2 (7.00–12.00) has eight word-picture and 40 sentence-completion items. Equivalent forms (1A and 2A) are available for each level. The **Manual** contains the usual advice on administering, scoring and statistical interpretation and the standardization procedure is described fully. Levels 1 and 2 were standardized in 1978 on samples of 1,500 children in the top infant to third-year junior range and a subsidiary smaller sample was used to provide fairly reliable reading ages up to 13.06.

As is often found with sentence-completion tests, reliability is high, both by internal consistency and test-retest. Correlations between Levels 1 and 2 ranged from .85 to .86 and correlations with the equivalent forms, 1A and 2A, from .81 to .94. Validity evidence is restricted to correlations expressing agreement with teachers' judgements (.73 to .89) and other reading tests (.71 to .91), although even this is thorough evidence compared to many other standardized sentence-completion tests.

The high standards and care with which the statistical development has been conducted are exemplary. In this respect the *Primary Reading Test* excels most other sentence-completion tests published for this age range. Relative recency of standardization, provision of norms for a wide age range and availability of equivalent forms further enhance its appeal. In practical terms, it is probably the most suitable choice for schools wishing to replace any of the more dated sentence-completion tests they may be using.

Nevertheless the *Primary Reading Test* has intrinsic limitations. The Manual states that it gives 'an overall assessment of the ability to apply reading skills for the understanding of words and simple sentences in the *early stages of learning to read*', (reviewer's italics). Yet, the Test is explicitly intended for use throughout the junior age range and the standardization emphasizes the second and third junior years in that both levels of the test are standardized for this age group. The Manual offers no resolution of this anomaly.

Reading Vocabulary Tests

Alan Brimer and Herbert Gross

1979

Education Evaluation Enterprises

Group; Objective; Standardized; 6.09–12.02; Standardized Scores, 'Scale Scores' (based on Rasch scaling); Timed, 30 minutes; Equivalent Forms (2); Consumable; UK.

The Tests are two forms of a conventional 36-item sentence-completion test designed to provide a global measure of reading vocabulary, 'understanding of individual words in the context of sentences', across a wide age range.

The items are printed on a single **test sheet** and a two-page **Administrative Manual** contains brief directions, a standardized score conversion table and a table for 'scale scores'. The latter system allows raw scores to be converted to a 20-point 'equal interval' scale. In essence this constitutes an 'absolute' measure of attainment and a score of, say, ten can be interpreted as being 'twice' as high as one of five. However little endeavour is made to explain this system to potential users of the tests.

No validity evidence is quoted although it is noted that Rasch analysis – the method used to derive the scale scores – led to removal of certain unsuitable trial items. It is not explained why these particular items proved to be unsuitable or in what sense the remaining items were more valid. Reliabilities by internal consistency are given in the .85 to .92 range and the test-retest correlations between forms are from .71 to .87. Only 500 children were used in the standardization and it is not claimed this was representative of the age groups concerned. The standardized score tables must thus be regarded as no more than a rough guide, particularly as the age columns are grouped in four-month intervals, possibly for economy of printing. The scale scores are perhaps less affected by the smallness of the sample.

The general limitations of sentence completion must apply to the *Reading Vocabulary Tests*. Beyond economy and the innovatory use of the Rasch scaling of scores there is little to recommend them. (An item referring to slaves cowering beneath their master's whip and 'barely surviving the punishment' seems distinctly unsavoury.)

Richmond Test of Basic Skills

**A.N. Hieronymus and E.F. Lindquist
(UK Edition compiled by Norman France and
Ian Fraser)**

1981

NFER-NELSON

Group; Standardized; 8.00–14.00; Standard Age
Scores, Percentiles, Stanines; Total for all tests is five
hours; Re-usable except for pupil answer sheets; USA;
Computer Marking Available.

This is a battery of tests to measure vocabulary,
reading, language, study skills and mathematics for
pupils between eight and 14 years. Each test is set at
six different levels to cover six school years. (junior
stage years two, three and four, secondary stage years
one, two and three). Although the test originated in
the USA the material has been completely anglicized
and standardized for use in Britain.

All test material is included in a **Pupil's Book** which
is non-expendable as pupils taking each test use
separate **answer sheets** – these have an optional
computer-scored form. A **Teacher's Guide** gives
instructions for the administration of each test, directions for scoring and interpretation of results, and
suggestions for follow-up work in which the Guide
suggests pupils should assume responsibility for their
own improvement.

The test package includes **scoring templates** to
facilitate marking, **Pupil Profile Charts** in both tabular
and a 'circular' form, a **Class Record Sheet** and a
Table of Norms booklet.

The tests are organized within the pupil's book as
follows:

Test V Vocabulary (multiple-choice synonym-
matching items)

Test R Reading Comprehension (multiple-choice
passage comprehension items)

Test L Language Skills (multiple-choice error-
detection tasks):
  L-1 : Spelling
  L-2 : Use of Capital Letters
  L-3 : Punctuation
  L-4 : Usage

Test W Work Study Skills:
  W-1 : Map Reading
  W-2 : Reading Graphs and Tables
  W-3 : Knowledge and Use of Reference
  Materials

Test M Mathematics Skills:
  M-1 : Mathematics Concepts
  M-2 : Mathematics Problem Solving

Timing and directions are the same for each level, thus
allowing different levels of the same test to be
administered within the same group, if required. Four
sessions are proposed for administering the whole
battery of tests, although they could be used separately.

For older pupils the sessions could be given on four
consecutive days, but for pupils in the junior school a
day's break between each session is recommended.
Under no circumstances should all of the tests be
administered in a single day.

Test content is carefully graded and clearly presented in multiple-choice format. Reading skills are
essential but no writing is required. Pupils answer
questions by filling in small spaces on the answer
sheets. Marking is facilitated by overlay acetate sheets
and scores are recorded on an individual pupil profile
and also on a class record sheet which helps to guide
further work in each skill area.

Standardization of the original tests was undertaken
in the USA and they were later modified for use in the
UK with piloting undertaken in 1974 with a sample of
700 children in primary and secondary schools. A
sample of 17,000 children in England, Wales, Scotland and Northern Ireland took the tests in the autumn
of 1974 to provide raw data on which the norms were
based and from which the test's reliabilities were
calculated.

Many teachers could feel confused on first examining these tests although practice would soon clarify
points of presentation. Of more concern is the possible
reaction of pupils when presented with such a
formidable set of tasks. Some prior explanation that by
no means all the material must be attempted would
seem desirable. Problems could also arise in the
transfer of attention between the pupil's book and the
accompanying answer sheets. Therefore, the proposed times for administering the tests, which are very
long, may well be further lengthened by preliminary
explanations for younger or slower pupils.

This set of tests seems to be more suited to the

milieu of classrooms in the USA where substantial amounts of objective testing are generally accepted more readily than in the UK. Generally, the mode of testing is excessively mechanical and the emphasis on identification of errors in orthography and usage in the Language Skills tests – whatever its statistical value – raises major issues of balance and content validity.

The Teacher's Guide presents a skill classification of the various subtests together with well-intentioned advice on using the test results in 'improving instruction' ('enrichen the curriculum generally' is one of the suggestions for improving vocabulary). While one would not dispute the general soundness of this advice much of it is self-evident and commonplace.

The Richmond tests do provide British schools with many of the advantages of a highly developed US-style attainment battery: comprehensive coverage of age (and curriculum?); low cost of recurrent use; computer-scoring; class and individual profiles; clarity of explanation and presentation; authoritative norming. Nevertheless, the worthwhileness of this battery of tests must be questioned in relation to the amount of time which is invested, unless such time is clearly justified by detailed curriculum planning. This would require careful consideration of the relevance of the test materials to work in school and considerable thought to the way in which the results were to be used.

Salford Sentence Reading Test

G.E. Bookbinder

1976

Hodder & Stoughton

Individual; Objective; Standardized; 6.10–11.09; Percentile and Standardized Scores; Untimed (approximately 5 minutes); Equivalent Forms (3); Re-usable; UK.

The test is designed to give an accurate and speedy assessment of reading attainment up to a reading age of 10:6. Its use is mainly for the primary stage of schooling.

Each form of the test consists of 13 sentences printed on a **testcard** in increasing order of difficulty. The size of print corresponds to the degree of difficulty.

The child can commence at any point of the test at which he is able to read the consecutive sentences without error. Testing stops when the child has completed the sentence in which he makes his sixth error. When a child is unable to produce a word after six or seven seconds, it is supplied by the teacher and an error is recorded.

Directions for administering the test and scoring are set out on the reverse side of the test card. An eight-page **Manual** provides detailed information about the construction and standardization of the test.

Bookbinder states that the test was constructed largely on a trial-and-error basis. Initial criteria used in grading the difficulty of sentences were an increase in word length and, to a lesser extent, the estimated unfamiliarity of the words in successive sentences.

The standardization was carried out on 20,000 children in the age range 6.09–11.09, all living in the Salford authority. Correlations are given for the Salford test compared with four individual reading tests, one group reading test and one English test. All the tests appear to be largely measuring the same ability as the Salford test in the given age ranges.

Although Bookbinder does not say so it would appear that he has taken the Holborn Reading Scale (q.v.) as a model. Given the popularity of the Holborn

Scale the Salford test has appeared at a time when an alternative to the Holborn was badly needed. It can be argued that reading ability of older junior children is more than a matter of oral fluency and accuracy. However, there are practical advantages in a test which can be quickly administered by a class teacher in order to check on the progress of individual pupils. The Salford test is certainly a great advance on tests which have previously been used in this relatively informal way.

Schonell Graded Word Reading Test R1

F.J. Schonell

1955

Oliver & Boyd

Individual; Objective; Restandardized 1972; 6.00–12.06; Reading Ages; Untimed (approximately 10 minutes); Re-usable; UK.

The *Graded Word Reading Test* is one of a group of four Schonell reading tests (R1, R2, R3, R4) first published in 1951. Unlike the other three it continues to be widely used although at the time of writing all the tests are officially out of print. It comprises 100 words which are presented in order of difficulty. The teacher has to decide the most appropriate point to start testing and continues with the test until the pupil fails to read ten successive words correctly.

The 1955 edition of the **Handbook of Instructions** for all four tests provided a simple formula for calculating the pupil's reading age and for obtaining a reading quotient based on the difference between chronological and reading ages.

The 1981 edition of the handbook includes new norms provided by Bookbinder. These are based on a sample of children attending schools in Salford, and give a reading age range from 6.00 to 11.06 years. By a process of extrapolation from the 7.00–11.06 sample, the reading age range is extended to 12.06 years. The NFER has published a further restandardization based on a sample of Cheshire children. Shearer, who carried out the testing, reports that his norms differed from those issued by the publishers. The difference between the two sets of norms should lead to caution in the way teachers interpret reading ages based on the Schonell test. Certainly, it cannot be recommended for use with pupils at the secondary stage of education.

At the primary stage, the test has had a long period of popularity but class teachers now have access to a much wider range of tests than those first devised by Schonell in the post-war years. The test is identical in format to that of the *Burt Word Reading Test* (q.v.) and is subject to exactly the same shortcomings, differing only in the selection of words to be read.

Judged against contemporary theories of reading and reading curriculum the continued use of either test is to be deplored. Repeated use of the test on the same children, either yearly or termly, is not unheard of and this merely increases the pointlessness of using the tests.

Test R2, *Simple Prose Reading Test,* consisted of a five-paragraph narrative entitled 'My Dog' to be read aloud by the child and gave reading ages for comprehension based on 15 simple oral questions, for speed and for accuracy. Test R3 *Silent Reading Test A* consisted of 18 short paragraphs each followed by a short objectively scored question. Reading ages were given from 6.09 to 12.00+. Test 4, *Silent Reading Test B* – which perhaps anticipated cloze procedure – consisted of 20 short passages from which two or three words had been deleted and replaced by blanks of uniform length. The missing words had to be chosen from multiple-choice alternatives at the end of each passage. Reading ages were given from 6.08 to 13.00+. These tests were all re-usable and R3 and R4 are probably still used occasionally. However, it is ironic that they failed to enjoy the popularity of the much inferior R1.

Slee 13+ Reading Test

Frank Slee

Undated

LDA

Group; Objective; Standardized; 13.00–14.06; Standardized Scores; Timed, 20 minutes; Consumable; UK.

Although undated, the Slee test appears to be of fairly recent origin. It is specifically intended for assessing reading comprehension at 13+ and as a screening and survey device in the middle of high school transition years. The author argues that few other tests are specifically designed to cover the range of reading abilities in this age group.

The test consists of 35 multiple-choice items printed in a 7-page **test booklet.** The items are based on a series of short passages – 'mini-excerpts' – followed by between one and three questions. The excerpts are usually single sentences taken from a variety of fictional and textbook sources. The use of real texts means that the language is less forced and bizarre than in many sentence-based reading tests. The author states that the items make various demands, including knowledge of word meanings, literal comprehension and drawing of inferences. However, the brevity of the texts means that many of the questions require an inferential form of response. The reader must derive information which would probably have been supplied explicitly in the full text from which the passage was excerpted. In this respect the test could be said to impose a rather artificial reading activity involving a certain amount of astuteness and 'detective work'. At the same time, there are many situations in which readers of 13+ are confronted with partial or inexplicit texts and the Slee test could be regarded as true to life in this sense.

The 7-page **Teacher's Manual** gives exact administration instructions and quotes a KR20 reliability of .88. Correlations with NFER Reading tests range from .71 to .81 and a correlation of .61 with a non-verbal IQ test is given. A sample of 1,600 children in nine metropolitan schools was used for standardization.

This is too restricted a group to constitute an authoritative national norm but is perhaps adequate as a criterion for comparison when testing in other metropolitan settings. Examination of the tables for converting raw scores to standardized scores brings into question the claim that the test will 'distinguish between pupils over the whole thirteen plus ability range'. Certainly, the Slee is not inferior to tests of comparable length in its discriminatory powers but in a test of only 35 items it is inevitable that small raw score differences will tend to correspond to large standardized score differences. In the case of the Slee Test only five or six raw score points separate the average children (standardized score, 100) from the superior readers (standardized score 115 plus). This rather crude capacity to differentiate between ability levels is the price paid for a relatively quick and economical test.

The demand for standardized reading assessment at 13+ has not been great in the past, although there is a case for more serious monitoring of literacy at this age level. How far it should be carried out using simple, easy measures like the Slee, rather than more elaborate means such as the *Edinburgh Reading Test Stage 4* (q.v.) is open to debate.

Southgate Group Reading Test 1 : Word Selection Test

Vera Southgate

1959 (Ninth Impression 1976)

Hodder & Stoughton

Group; Objective; Standardized; 6.00–7.06 (up to 14.00 for slower learners); Reading Ages; Untimed (approximately 20 minutes); Equivalent Forms (3); Consumable; UK.

This word-selection test has three forms and is intended for use by class teachers. It was designed to fill a gap which existed in the UK for the assessment of pupils with reading ages of less than eight years and is particularly intended for use with children between six and seven and a half years.

The consumable **test booklets** have four sides of word selection exercises, 30 on each, some relating to pictures, which are ringed by the child as the teacher gives each target word. The **Manual** has 23 pages, setting out the purpose of the test, general instructions for administration and marking, a table of norms for the conversion of scores into reading ages and information on the construction and standardization of the test.

The test was constructed during five years of work, during which 676 items were devised and tried out with six- to seven-year-olds and older children with lower reading ability. Test-retest reliability is .96 and the three forms are also highly intercorrelated. Validity was established by comparing results with teachers' estimates of reading ability and by the correlations (ranging from .87 to .94) between raw scores and individual oral tests available at the time. Standardization was carried out in Worcester, with every child in LEA schools aged 5.08 years to 8.01 years, numbering 2,337 in all.

This is a straightforward test which is easy to administer and which will quickly produce a list of reading ages for a class of relatively young children. The amount of time invested is likely to be considerably less than that required for individual assessment and results are probably as reliable. While such information is extremely limited in its usefulness for making curriculum decisions, for situations where reading ages are demanded, this test seems to provide information with minimum encroachment into teaching time. However, the norms are now very dated and more recently standardized alternatives are available.

Southgate Group Reading Test 2: Sentence Completion Test

Vera Southgate

1962 (Fifth impression 1972)

Hodder & Stoughton

Group; Objective; Standardized; 7.00–8.11 (also older slow learners); Reading Ages, Percentiles; 15 minutes; Equivalent Forms (2); Consumable; UK.

This test is consecutive with Test 1 but with a slight overlap. It is concerned with the reading skills which extend from those required by infant reading schemes to a reading age of 9.00–9.06 and is most useful for pupils in the first two years of the junior stage of education.

The two parallel forms allow for class-group testing and for re-testing at a later stage. Each form is colour coded for easy recognition and each uses the same practice examples. The four-page **test booklets** each contain 42 sentences which are completed by the child drawing a ring round the correct choice out of five. In each case, it is the final word of the sentence which is chosen. The **Manual** gives concise information about the purposes, administration and marking, norms and construction.

Validity and reliability were estimated from results of 253 children who took both forms of the test, together with an NFER sentence reading test and the *Schonell Graded Word Reading Test* (q.v.), giving correlation coefficients between .82 and 0.97. Standardization was carried out in Worcester, as was Test 1, with every child in LEA schools aged between 7.00 and 10.11 (3,751 children).

This is a straightforward test which is easy to administer and which gives reading ages and percentiles with a minimum of administration and marking. It has limitations which are inherent in all sentence-completion tests and like Test 1, is dated in standardization.

SPAR (Spelling and Reading) Tests

D. Young

1976

Hodder & Stoughton

Group; Objective; Standardized; Junior–15.00 plus; Reading Ages, Spelling Ages, Quotients (Standardized scores; 7.0–15.11); Timed (Reading), 13 minutes; Equivalent Forms (2, Reading) (10, Spelling); Consumable; UK.

The SPAR Tests are intended to assess the progress towards literacy of children of a wide range of ability in the first year of junior school and of less able pupils up to the age of 15.11.

The Reading Test follows the same formula as that of the author's *Group Reading Test* (q.v.) and the marking templates for that test can be used for the two forms of the SPAR reading test:

Picture-word matching, (15 items). The pupil is required to select from a group of 4/5 words one which matches the given outline picture.

Sentence completion, (30 items). Incomplete sentences are presented. For each sentence the pupil has to select the appropriate word from a group of six in order to complete the sentence.

The 32-page **Manual** gives clear directions for administering the reading tests – those for spelling are somewhat more complicated. The method of converting raw scores to attainment ages and quotients is described as well as the process of standardization. At the junior age range, the norms are based on a group of schools known to be representative of the national pattern of achievement in NFER and Moray House tests. For the reading sample, the number of junior children was 3,797. The norms at the secondary level are based on a sample of 936 children; the method of calibration from nationally standardized tests is not, however, described. Various indices of reliability and validity are presented for four groups of junior pupils and for one group at the secondary level.

The **pupils' test forms** differ from those of most group tests in that they are contained on one sheet. This is achieved by placing the test items very close together and could present difficulties for some pupils unless special care is taken in administering the test.

The tests are designed mainly for use at the junior stage and it is at this level where they have the greatest degree of reliability and validity. Although the author says that the tests can be used for pupils of less ability up to the age of 15.11, they cannot be recommended for general use at the secondary stage. For less able pupils individual tests would be more appropriate.

For the SPAR Spelling Tests, the teacher can construct ten parallel forms without any overlap in content, and a far larger number with partial overlap. This is accomplished by systematically selecting pairs of words from two 'banks' of words printed in the Manual. The words are then dictated to the children in the context of appropriate sentences devised by the teacher. The standardization of the tests was based mainly on the same group of children as for the reading tests.

Using the SPAR Reading and Spelling Tests for a whole class of children may be more helpful in the consideration of individual differences in these two aspects of literacy. In particular, it may be possible to identify contrasting groups; children who are equally poor at both skills and the average readers who are relatively poor spellers.

Transitional Assessment : English

1978

NFER-NELSON

Group; Partly Objective; Unstandardized; Primary to Secondary Transfer Age; 'Stages'; Untimed; Consumable; UK.

The test materials consist of eight 'modules' or sub-tests of reading and writing skills. They form part of a larger 'bank' of test modules designed to form a standard framework for passing on information about attainment on transfer from primary to secondary school. The materials were developed in the London Borough of Hillingdon and should be viewed as an approach to large-scale LEA assessment needs, rather than as free-standing attainment tests for classroom use.

Modules **1** to **4** consist of free essay tasks on Autobiographical, Descriptive, Explanatory/Factual and Story Writing themes, respectively. **Module 5** is a sentence-writing task in which grammatically correct sentences must be written using 12 stem words or phrases. **Module 6,** Punctuation, requires a poorly punctuated passage to be written out correctly. **Module 7** contains three 'cloze' technique passages from the NFER *Reading Level Tests* (q.v.) and **Module 8** is a conventional continuous prose comprehension task. Performance is classified according to four stages, starting at a 'below Stage 1' category. A standard **profile sheet** is used to record this for each task. These stages are, loosely, criterion-referenced scores. Allocation to stages depends upon specified aspects of performance. For the more objective modules the stages correspond to score levels or answers to particular sets of questions, but for the essay tasks the process involves subjective impressions, albeit following some general guidelines prepared to 'improve inter-school reliability'. For example, a criterion of Stage 1 performance is use of 'extremely mundane or repetitious' language.

No validity or reliability data are given in the Manual, which is intended essentially as a guide to using and scoring the Modules. However, the test formats employed have generally proved satisfactory in this respect.

The aims of providing secondary schools with some sort of objective measure of student attainment and of providing primary schools with the tests to give these measures are probably ones that many teachers would applaud. One must ask, however, how 'objective' can these tests be? All too often the testing and marking of English has suffered from the fact that it is easy to pinpoint errors in grammar, punctuation and spelling and far harder to do much about the other aspects of writing.

These materials do not entirely confront these problems but there is evidence that in some areas at least, good practice has been upheld and bad practice avoided. For instance, punctuation and sentence construction are here tested separately from extended writing and there are four different writing tasks which can be tackled in any order with no pre-set time limit (unless the teacher decides on one). Presumably the types of task set are meant to represent a fair cross-section of primary school/early secondary school tasks – they certainly correspond with the tasks set by well-known researchers in the field of writing development. The very balance of six tests for writing compared with two for reading shows the importance and complexity that is now recognized in relation to written work in schools.

But tests are still tests. Teachers, though they are encouraged to give details of their own criteria for marking will still be heavily influenced by the criteria used in the guidance notes and the tests are still of the 'one-off' nature. There is only one chance to give a successful answer to each module and it is for an unknown audience – as contextless and lacking in clear criteria as most tests usually are.

One other point – considering the richness of data that would emerge from the completion of the modules the allocation to one of three stages seems a puny outcome.

Wide-span Reading Test (Revised Edition)

Alan Brimer and Herbert Gross

1972

NFER-NELSON

Group; Objective; Standardized; 7.00–14.11; Standardized Scores, Percentiles, 'Diagnostic Indicators', 'Nominal Scale'; Timed, 30 minutes; Equivalent Forms (2); Re-usable; UK.

The Wide-span is described as a test of reading comprehension and can be used either as a general measure of reading attainment or to diagnose certain aspects of reading difficulty.

Each form of the test contains eighty items consisting of two unrelated sentences. The second sentence contains a blank, indicating a missing word which has also been used in the first sentence. The child has to identify the target word and write it on a separate answer sheet. Items are steeply graded in difficulty to cover a wide ability range. Accordingly, separate starting points are designated for successive age groups. For example, fourth-year secondary pupils begin at the 57th item. The test is strictly timed to 30 minutes so that younger children are not forced to tackle an excessive number of items.

Total raw scores are converted to standardized scores in a two-step process – perhaps less convenient than the more usual standardized score tables – using a conversion table and a separate age adjustment table. These are presented separately for each form and for first and second occasions of testing. The latter elaboration is necessary as children in the standardization sample scored consistently higher when re-tested on the relevant equivalent form of the test. Detailed instructions are also available for categorizing wrong answers as 'Decoding', 'Linguistic' or 'Vocabulary' errors. This is certainly an advance on conventional sentence-completion testing, but the advice given on interpreting these diagnostic indicators is general, if not vague. Certainly, no evidence is given for the clinical or practical value of such scores. One is left with the impression that this was an ingenious idea which the authors failed to follow-up in any detail. Reference is also made to a 'nominal scale' for the 'highest level of the child's effective functioning'. It is, in fact, based on the last raw score point at which three consecutive items were correct. If a child fails to attain a nominal scale score because the pattern of correct answers was sporadic – perhaps where a poor reader has relied upon guessing – testing can be repeated at a lower level starting point. No explanation is given as to how these scores are to be further used.

The test was standardized on over 7,000 children in a nationally representative sample of schools, and test–retest reliability based on inter-form correlations ranges from .89 to .95. No validity evidence is presented although this would be highly desirable in view of the unusual format of the test items. However, in *Extending Beginning Reading,* by Vera Southgate, Helen Arnold and Sandra Johnson (Heinemann Educational Books, 1982) a correlation of .81 with the *Southgate Group Reading Test 2* (q.v.) is reported.

The Manual claims that the Wide-span measures both decoding and more complex linguistic processes necessary to reading comprehension. It also implies that the 'contrived, tortuous and tautologous' nature of the second sentences is necessary to its functions of permitting 'hypotheses about the character of the missing word to be tested'. It is certainly plausible that good readers would be better than poor readers at jumping through the somewhat strange hoops presented by Wide-span but, as in conventional multiple-choice sentence-completion tests, the task itself has little in common with purposeful reading. If it could be shown that the diagnostic indicators available with this form of testing were of practical remedial value such reservations about the two-sentence format would carry much less weight. Interestingly, this possibility was not explored in the Extending Beginning Reading research. It is certainly one that a teacher could usefully consider as a piece of classroom research. However, as a general routine testing device it has little advantage over more conventional tests.

Section II:
Diagnostic and Classroom Tests

Some of the tests and procedures reviewed in this section are standardized in the same way as the attainment tests and reliability and validity data are also given for many of them. In these respects they can be evaluated along similar lines to tests in Section I. However, closer consideration should be given to their direct value as teaching tools and this may outweigh the statistical considerations. A number of the tests are by intention or implication 'criterion-referenced'. This means they measure reading in terms of the specific content or skills that have been mastered, not in terms of norms or average standards. This is particularly the case with tests of phonic skills.

Many of the tests are concerned with the 'diagnosis' of reading difficulty and there is a diverse, if not bewildering, array of ways in which this can be done. Are some of the materials better or more effective than others? As in the case of Section I it is easier to indicate which tests should *not* be used than which should. In some cases reviewers advise categorically against using the materials under review. Nevertheless, equally good, but differing, choices remain. The final choice must be personal, perhaps taking economy of time and purchase into account. Above all, each test has its own in-built limitations and testing alone cannot give a comprehensive diagnosis. *None of the materials reviewed in this section are substitutes for the teacher's professional knowledge and judgement.*

Tests in this section tend to be more complex in composition than those in Section I. As before, individual components are indicated in bold face but many of the materials require time to be spent in familiarization before use.

Assessment of Reading Ability

Don Labon

1973

Education Department, County Hall, Chichester, West Sussex PO19 1RF

Individual; Partly Objective; Unstandardized; 5.00–9.00; Untimed; Re-usable; UK.

Assessment of Reading Ability is a short booklet (currently priced at 50p) describing procedures and sub-tests for classroom diagnosis of reading difficulty in the primary school.

The procedure commences with administration of Schonell's *Graded Word Reading Test* (q.v.) which is printed in the booklet for convenience. At the teacher's discretion subsequent tests are selected to identify reading difficulties more closely:

1. Word Pairs (for reading ages 5.00 to 6.00). This is similar to the *Wepman Auditory Discrimination Test*. The teacher reads aloud twelve pairs of words and the child must say whether they are 'same' or 'different'. (The Wepman is not normally available to schools; it differs mainly from the above test in having some normative information attached to it.)

2. Odd-Man-Out (for reading ages 6.00 to 7.00). In this test the teacher reads aloud a group of four words and the child must pick out the one which does not rhyme with the other three.

3. Word Building (for reading ages 7.00 plus). This is an oral reading test of 45 nonsense words containing common phonic blends and digraphs, most of the range of vowel sounds and some letter grouping conventions.

4. Letter Sounds (for low scorers on Word Building). The teacher is directed to test knowledge of letter sounds using either home-made letter cards or published materials.

The booklet contains advice on remedial activities for children who perform badly on these tests and further suggestions are contained in other booklets published by West Sussex LEA, including *Phonics* and *Teaching Non-Readers*.

The tests are designed for more or less informal use by teachers and no claims are made for statistical validation. However, it is reported that the materials resulted from development trials by 29 teachers with a total of 145 children of reading ages between 5.00 and 9.00 plus. Median scores are given for children in the original study but no other technical details are given.

The procedures have the advantages of simplicity and informality and they would be suitable as a modest and manageable means of introducing teachers to the assessment of reading difficulty. The materials were developed by school psychologists with local needs in mind. Yet, the booklet seems to have attracted more general interest than the author may have originally intended. It would thus be unfair to judge the materials by strict technical or theoretical criteria. Indeed, many of the diagnostic procedures reviewed elsewhere in this volume are open to criticism on grounds of excessive complexity. While it could be said that the West Sussex approach goes too far to the opposite extreme it is evident that it meets a need for guidance on classroom diagnosis in a way not catered for in larger-scale publications. At a current cost of 50 pence the booklet is definitely the most cost effective form of diagnostic assessment reviewed in this volume!

Assessing Reading Difficulties

Lynette Bradley

1980

Macmillan Education

Individual; Objective; Unstandardized; 5.00–8.00+; Untimed (5 minutes); Consumable (Test Sheets); UK.

This 'diagnostic and remedial approach' to reading difficulty aims to assess the learner's capacity to categorize words according to sound. The author argues that reading difficulty often involves inability to generalize from one written word to another by recognition of common elements within them. The tests aim to provide a means of identifying and remedying this difficulty.

The materials consist of a 32-page **booklet** and a **Test Sheet.** The first 14 pages of the booklet reviews research into reading difficulty. The author's own research is particularly emphasized. This explored differences in performance between normal and poor readers on three experimental tasks, one of which constitutes the basis of the main published test.

The testing commences with an informal nursery rhyme task and develops into an odd-man-out game, designed to prepare for the test proper. This consists of 24 orally administered trials in which the child must identify the word which 'doesn't go' in a set of four, e.g. hat/mat/**fun**/cat. In the first eight words the difference is in the first sound of the target word, in the second eight the middle sound is different and in the last set the final sound is different. Performance is recorded on the individual Test Sheet which provides space for brief general comments. Acceptable levels of error are given for age groups 5.00 to 8.00 and the last eight pages of the booklet outline some remedial procedures designed to develop generalization of categories skills.

The booklet refers to trials with 400 five-year-olds, but it is unclear how far the acceptable score levels reflect any kind of standardization research. The validity of the test procedure and these score levels would seem to rest more upon the results of the author's own research.

Although Lynette Bradley's materials are useful in alerting teachers to the possibility that a child has difficulty in the processes of generalizing and organizing written language they hardly provide an overall solution to the problem of assessing reading difficulty.

A fully informed diagnostic approach would take account of many factors and processes additional to those highlighted by Dr. Bradley. The publication of the materials in this apparently self-contained form is thus perhaps misleading. The test itself could, however, provide a useful addition to other existing batteries, particularly the West Sussex *Assessment of Reading Ability* (q.v.) materials or the *Infant Reading Tests* (q.v.).

Aston Index

M.J. Newton and M.E. Thomson

1976*

LDA

Individual; Partly Objective; Partly Standardized; 5.06–14.00; Raw Score Norms; Untimed; Consumable Record Forms; UK.

The *Aston Index* is a battery of diagnostic tests and procedures designed for use by class teachers. The Index can be used at two levels. Level 1 use involves screening of children 5.06–7.00, to identify those who may encounter subsequent learning difficulties. Level 2 use is for the diagnosis of older children, up to 14.00, who are experiencing actual difficulties in reading and writing. Much of the Level 1 test material is also used at Level 2. The Index was developed by researchers at the University of Aston and there are a number of published accounts of the associated research and development work, particularly M.J. Newton, M.E. Thomson and I. Richards in *Readings in Dyslexia: A Study Text to Accompany the Aston Index* (LDA, 1978).

Although the Index has its origins in dyslexia research it can be used in its published form without necessarily referring to the specific concept of dyslexia.

There are sixteen tests in the battery, some of which are designated for use at only one of the two levels. Instructions for testing, and in some cases the test cards, are presented in a **Test Cards Manual.** Separate **cards, booklets** and **test sheets** are provided as necessary for other tests. The materials are as follows:

Test 1, Picture Recognition (10 items). The child must name objects depicted on each of ten cards. (Level 1 only).

Test 2, Aston Vocabulary Scale (26 items). The child must give spoken definitions of up to 26 verbally named objects. Raw scores can be converted to equivalent ages.

Test 3, *The Goodenough Draw-a-Man Test*. The child is instructed to draw a picture of a man or a woman. The result is scored out of 50, using a checklist of features to be presented. This is converted to a Mental Age scale.

Test 4, Copying Geometric Designs (4 items). Four geometric designs (circle, square, triangle and diamond) must be copied, three times each, from example cards.

Test 5, *Schonell Graded Word Reading Test* (q.v.) (reproduced in the Test Cards book).

Test 6, *Schonell Graded Spelling Test* (reproduced in the Test Cards book).

Test 7, Child's Laterality (10 tasks). A series of practical activities are prescribed in which the child must handle various objects (not supplied) and perform motor tasks in a way designed to elicit any sign of inconsistency in laterality – the preference for using the left or right limb or perceptual organ.

Test 8, Copying Name. The child is instructed to write his/her name. (Level 1 only)

Test 9, Free Writing. A piece of free writing must be obtained. This is scored out of 10, according to specified guidelines. (Level 2 only)

Test 10, Visual Sequential Memory (Pictorial) (10 items). The child must reproduce a pictorial sequence presented by selecting and ordering the relevant picture cards. Mirror-image examples of the objects are included amongst the cards so that any tendency towards confused orientation can be noted.

Test 11, Auditory Sequential Memory (20 items). The tester dictates a series of digits which must be repeated by the child, ten in the order given, ten in reverse order. Knowledge of common sequences, such as days of the week, is also tested.

Test 12, Sound Blending (20 items). Target words are pronounced at the rate of one sound per second and the child must blend them orally.

Test 13, Visual Sequential Memory (Symbolic) (10 items). Memory for pictorially-presented sequence is tested, using abstract symbols, in a format similar to that of Test 10.

Test 14, Sound Discrimination (20 items). The child must repeat two words spoken by the tester. Some of the pairs contain the same word and the child must say whether they are the same, or different.

---

*Subsequent to the completion of this review a revised edition of the *Aston Index* has been published. This includes a further visual discrimination test and some re-ordering and re-numbering of the tests. The revisions do not alter the overall evaluation offered in this review, however.

Test 15, Grapheme/Phoneme Correspondence. Letters of the alphabet must be named and sounded. The letters are printed in upper and lower case in the Test Cards book.

Test 16, Grapho-Motor Test (12 items). A pattern of connected loops must be copied on a **Test Form.** Successive trials are made using left-to-right and right-to-left starting points alternately. (Level 2 only)

Performance on the tasks is recorded in a six-page **recording form.** On the last two pages profiles are completed for 'general underlying ability and attainment' (based on Tests 1, 2, 3, 5 and 6) and for the 'performance items' (Tests 10, 11, 12, 13 and 14). Norms of the latter are indicated by feint lines on the profile table. A **Handbook** is provided, in addition to the Test Card instructions, which describes the overall purpose of the Index and gives detailed advice on scoring and interpretation. It includes additional normative information although it is stressed that this is a general guideline and should not be too rigidly interpreted. 'Split half' reliabilities for some of the tests are given and these appear satisfactory although it was not thought relevant to study reliability of the 'more qualitative' tests. Validity evidence includes correlations between Index scores and attainment two years later. Although some of these are low or insignificant the overall pattern of results is satisfactory for a longitudinal validation study of this kind. A short **supplementary pamphlet** notes various other materials produced by LDA which may be relevant to performance on some of the Index tests.

The decision of the constructors and publishers to make a test of this sort available to class teachers is controversial. Individual psychological test batteries are the traditional province of the trained psychologist. Indeed, many of the sub-tests are modelled on tests normally restricted to use by school and clinical psychological services. It would be highly desirable to confer with a school's psychological service before adopting the *Aston Index* into a school's assessment programme. However, professional boundaries are often less strictly preserved than hitherto and many psychologists would certainly welcome interest in the Index by teachers as a useful initial basis for cooperation and liaison.

How effectively does the Index translate or package the expertise of the educational psychologist for classroom use? There are immediate and practical problems. The tests take some time to administer and many class teachers might have difficulty in finding time to give them to even one or two children. There is also the question of how far teachers would be prepared to spend time familiarizing themselves with the materials, developing administration skills and in the desirable – if not essential – recommended background reading. In fact, a fairly full self-training programme is required. Advisory and remedial teachers might well have greater incentive and scope to do this than would general class teachers.

By intention, the Index follows established theories of learning and language difficulty and established patterns of clinical practice. The individual tests certainly draw the teacher's attention, in general terms, to potential specific sources of difficulty. Sometimes there are flaws in the details of the tests. For example, the Auditory Sequential Memory Test is not necessarily measuring auditory encoding – some children use *visual* imagery as a learning strategy on such tasks. Also, the Index's reference to 'restricted' use of language suggests too much credence may be given to questionable deficit theories of language difficulty. The use of the outdated Schonell Reading and Spelling Tests is also disappointing.

More serious questions surround the Index's emphasis upon processes which precede or preclude success in learning to read. Certainly, some careful and sophisticated research studies were carried out to demonstrate the predictive validity of the tests. However, this does not 'prove' that remedial activities designed to strengthen or alter the processes measured will lead to reading success, although they may be a sensible point to start in the absence of any other guidance. This reservation apart, it must be acknowledged that the Aston Index currently presents methods of in-depth diagnosis for teachers – should they wish to use them – in a more accessible form than any other commercially published test kit. Ultimately, the *Barking Project* materials (q.v.) may prove to be a better choice – they are potentially both simpler and more comprehensive – for teachers concerned with diagnosing severe difficulties. It would also be worth asking whether the *Aston Portfolio* (q.v.) or the *Macmillan Diagnostic Reading Pack* (q.v.) do not offer alternatives better suited to many schools' needs.

The Bangor Dyslexia Test

T.R. Miles

1982

LDA

Individual; Unstandardized; 7.00+; Consumable; UK.

The origins of this test are fully described in T.R. Miles's *Dyslexia: The Pattern of Difficulties* (Granada Press, 1983). This text was not available at the time of reviewing and the comments that follow must be regarded as tentative and provisional.

The test consists mainly of a series of performance tasks designed to identify possible cases of dyslexia. It is intended for use by a variety of relevant professions in addition to teachers and educational psychologists. Professor Miles associates 'dyslexia' with persistent difficulty with spelling and a 'constitutionally caused' inability to 'process other kinds of symbolic material'. This is reflected in the main sections of the test which are presented on a single **test sheet** containing both specific instructions and space for recording responses:

1. Left–right (body parts). The subject is instructed to point to or touch designated parts of his own or the tester's body. This will indicate any confusion over left–right differentiation.

2. Repeating polysyllabic words. Five multisyllable words are spoken by the tester to be repeated by the subject.

3. Subtraction. The subject must perform six mental arithmetic subtraction tasks.

4. Tables. At least three multiplication tables must be recited from memory.

5 and 6. Months forwards; Months reversed. The months of the year must be recited in both normal and reversed sequence.

7 and 8. Digits forwards; Digits reversed. These consist of two conventional digital memory-span tests.

9. b-d confusion. The test must note whether the subject has a history of confusing 'b' and 'd'.

10. Familial incidence. Where possible it must be ascertained whether there is a family history of difficulty with written language or with tasks such as those included in the test.

A seven-page **manual** provides additional 'notes on what to look out for' while administering the test. Great emphasis is placed upon qualitative observation of performance in addition to making a numerical tally of errors. Both types of information are used to code the results of each section as either 'dyslexia positive', 'dyslexia negative' or 'zero' (ambiguous). This coding procedure includes certain adjustments to take account of normal maturational differences. The author is reluctant to specify exact criteria for identifying someone as dyslexic although tables are given to show differences in mean scores of dyslexic and control subjects. It is stressed that overall impression, 'good sense' and a 'feel' for incongruous responses are important in diagnosis.

There is much to be said for avoiding rigid prescription in preference for clinical judgement. Further, the author advises that the test is to be used as part of a 'wider assessment' and is not 'a means of definitive diagnosis'. Nevertheless, the Bangor test arouses some unease. It is temptingly easy to use in comparison to other means of diagnosing severe and specific difficulty with written language. There is thus a danger that it will come to be used in isolation by those who do not have time to carry out more searching assessments. This is potentially a large group. Also, the author's reassurance that little is lost by incorrectly referring someone for further testing for dyslexia is not entirely convincing.

No reliability information is presented, and validity data are confined to two tables comparing performance of dyslexic and control groups. These certainly indicate a tendency for the former group to do worse on the test, but the difference is far from perfect. Such results may justify the use of the test as an exploratory instrument for the further study of dyslexia but they are a questionable basis for adopting the test for routine clinical use. The *Aston Index* (q.v.) would seem a sounder basis for such testing.

It must be repeated that this review is based on partial information and the comments are the reviewer's initial impressions. A definitive evaluation of the Bangor test would involve a definitive evaluation of the associated research and, indeed, contemporary concepts of dyslexia. This is beyond the scope of the current review. However, judged as a free-standing test on the basis of the materials provided the *Bangor Dyslexia Test* cannot really be recommended. One could certainly not support its use by anyone who had not taken the trouble to study the associated book.

Barking Reading Project (University College London Revision) Book 1 : Assessment

1980

London Borough of Barking and Dagenham Schools' Psychological Service

Individual; Objective; Standardized; 6.00–11.00; Profile; Timed, 45 minutes; Re-usable (9-page consumable record sheet); UK.

The Barking Project provides an integrated approach to the assessment and monitoring of reading within a diagnostic frame of reference. The Assessment package is used to establish a level of attainment and to pinpoint areas of weakness prior to the implementation of an individual assignment programme. The Barking Project includes a large number of activities and worksheets for remedial follow-up to the assessment procedures although this review concentrates upon the latter.

Book One: Assessment. This gives details of the Project and an overview of the 11 areas covered in Assessment, with chapters on each of the nine skills and two checklists. The smaller **Assessment Manual** gives directions for administration in the nine areas which constitute the profile summary and skill profile on the **record sheet.**

1. Word retention. Two words, printed on a Polyart card, are taught to the child through visual inspection/writing. When the card is held to the light the target words are visible but they cannot be seen when the card is flat. The child must inspect the words, lay the card flat and write them out on the card and then check the attempt by holding the card up again. At the end of the test the child is required to recall/relearn the words.

2. Concepts and Vocabulary of Reading Instruction, (21 items). Understanding of common terms used in reading instructions is tested using a special **reading book.** (Nine additional concepts are unscored.)

3. Letter Knowledge, (24 items). The child has to name and sound lower case letters (omitting 'q' and 'x') presented on a card.

4. Visual Sequential Memory, (8 items). A test of sequential memory for letter combinations varying from three to six letters in length.

5. Visual Matching, (30 items, ten in each of three categories, word forms, orientation and detail). The child is required to select one from five (word forms) or four (orientation and detail) similar stimuli to match an initial stimulus presentation.

6. Sounds in Words, (20 items). The child is required to indicate in which of a pair of named stimulus pictures a specified sound appears.

7. Auditory Sequential Memory, (12 items). The child must repeat four-letter words broken down into two, three and four segments. (Segments are weighted in scoring.)

8. Sound Blending, (12 items). The child must synthesize four-letter words presented as two, three and four segments into the whole word. (Segments are weighted in scoring.)

9. Grapho-motor, (8 items, final item unscored). The child is required to perform increasingly difficult hand/eye coordination tasks. Two of the items are timed.

10. Attitude and Motivation: Checklist 1, (29 items). Five areas are covered concerning: What motivates? Who teaches? Where? When? and How? are covered. Teachers are required to tick boxes which apply.

11. Early Phonic Knowledge, (48 items). Nine phonic categories are sampled; letter sounds ('q' and 'x' are excluded), common digraphs, consonant-vowel-consonant blends, b/d confusion, double consonant endings, 'ee' and 'oo', end blends, magic 'e' and initial blends.

The Barking Reading Project was developed from an initial pilot study with four junior schools, in 1975, followed by subsequent field trials, to its present level of sophistication. Monitoring and modification continue and the Project should not currently be seen as a static 'finished product'.

The rejection of a global reading age and the adoption of a diagnostic model which views reading as a synthesis of interrelated and complementary skills has resulted in an assessment package which, whilst comprehensive, may appear, at first sight, daunting to the class teacher in comparison with more familiar tests of reading. However, careful perusal of the assessment book should dispel initial fears. There is a complete explanatory chapter assigned to each measure, describing the skill, outlining its relation to other skills, the effects of deficit in the child and the procedures for assessment.

The emphasis upon classroom practicalities in assessment and remediation is commendable, although from the statistical standpoint it would be useful if further details concerning reliability and validity could be provided, either as appendices to the current assessment book or in the form of a separate booklet. It would be interesting, for example, to be able to examine the ways in which the nine areas making up the skill profile are related to one another and to the two additional checklists. At present, the user must trust to the (unknown) procedures of the research team.

These omissions in reporting data analysis do not detract from the overall practical impact of the Project, which is impressive in its scope and which reflects much of the philosophy of applied psychologists working in the field. (See PRESLAND, J., (1982). 'Applying Psychology to Teaching Reading', *Division of Educational and Child Psychology: Occasional Papers*, Vol. 6, No. 1, pp. 14–23. British Psychological Society.) Thus, while we have little information on construct validity, the face validity of the measures, coupled with claims for 'spectacular gains in reading

age . . .' over five years of field trials, is high. There are, however, some minor criticisms at this level. For example, the Word Retention Test requires the child to learn two words which appear on the record sheet and on a specially produced card. A possible confounding feature here is that the words appear in a different order on the record sheet and on the card.

There is little indication regarding the age range covered. The book on assessment refers to a pilot study in four junior schools with children whose reading skills were '. . . more than two years behind their chronological ages . . .', yet a table of notional ability levels at the back of the assessment manual gives provisional norms based upon '. . . the scores of children aged 6–7 years'. Further details of sampling would clear up this confusion.

One final point on presentation. In general the assessment book and materials are well produced; the assessment manual, however, is rather poorly printed and the typeface not as readable as it might be.

As a diagnostic, skill-based approach to the assessment and remediation of reading problems, the Barking Reading Project appears highly promising. It is to be hoped that further development will result in a revision which includes technical details of statistical analysis and sampling and attends to aspects of presentation. Like the more modest *Assessment of Reading Ability* booklet (q.v.) from West Sussex, the Barking Project started as a response to immediate local needs but it seems possible that it will soon be available in a commercially-published form, and this is to be welcomed.

Cassell's Linked English Tests

D.S. Higgins

1977

Cassell

Group; Objective; Standardized (Attainment Tests); 9.06–12.06; Standardized Scores; Timed Attainment Tests (35 minutes), Untimed Diagnostic Tests; Equivalent Forms (2); Consumable; UK.

These materials provide a self-contained programme of assessment, diagnosis and linked workbooks. The programme is intended for general teaching in the junior school rather than specialized remedial work. The concept of 'diagnosis' is thus used to apply to the identification of strength and weakness in more or less average children rather than of the markedly backward child.

The programme consists of an **Attainment Test** (Form A or B) of 94 items covering Spelling, 'Linguistics', Vocabulary, Punctuation and Comprehension, five corresponding **Diagnostic Tests,** and five matching **Workbooks.** Results of the Attainment Test are used to direct pupils to appropriate Diagnostic Tests and these in turn indicate sections of the corresponding Workbooks to be studied. The general principle is thus one of individualized prescription. Separate **Administrative Manuals** are provided for Attainment and Diagnostic Tests. The former contains instructions for giving and marking the tests, conversion tables and general advice on using a **Marking Grid** – printed in each pupil's test booklet – to determine strengths and weaknesses. The Diagnostic Test Manual outlines procedures for giving each test, discusses the skills involved and suggests relevant teaching activities. Some Diagnostic Tests are accompanied by further grids to allow matching with sections in the Workbooks.

The materials concerned with Spelling, Vocabulary, Punctuation and Comprehension reflect fairly standard conceptions of these processes. 'Linguistics' is a less common categorization which the author adopted 'only after much hesitancy'. It subsumes nine miscellaneous aspects of language usage, including use of tense, pronouns, compound sentences, judgement of various stylistic and rhetorical features of language and aspects of syntax and construction.

No evidence for test reliability or validity is presented, although the provision of norms for the Attainment Tests and reference to preliminary field trials invite evaluation by statistical criteria. At the same time, there is insufficient information to do this thoroughly. This leaves the impression that item analysis and standardization may have been somewhat crude or makeshift. There are certainly other standardized tests covering many of the same skills for which details of standardization are presented much more convincingly.

However, the overall model of integrated assessment and teaching is an advance over many other standardized tests. The general approach has much to offer the class teacher who wishes to work systematically on literacy skills and is prepared to tailor diagnosis and learning to individual and small group needs. At the same time, for such integrated approaches to be effective two key criteria must be met: the effectiveness of the links between testing and teaching must be proven and the processes and skills to be learned must be of relevance to overall language development.

The advice on using the tests and workbooks is clear and specific. However, the criterion scores for directing pupils to diagnostic tests and to workbooks appear to be based on intuition and judgement rather than empirical trials – teaching experience with the materials might indicate need for revision. The workbooks themselves differ little from many other free-standing publications and in places they are mechanical and repetitive. In effect, as a follow-on to the preceding assessment and diagnosis they are unlikely to have any special or unique virtues. The five-part model of language is similar to those found in other tests of English or 'English Progress'. Like these, it can be criticized for its narrowness and for lack of evidence that it is really the best basis for developing competence in 'real life' reading and writing tasks. In many respects the materials seem distinctly 'old-fashioned'. Nevertheless, within these limitations there is much to be commended. Explanation is full and the advice is often sound – the sections on spelling have benefited particularly from a contribution by Charles Cripps.

So few tests developed in the UK seek to integrate testing and teaching – particularly outside the realms of initial or remedial teaching – that the *Linked English Tests* must be given serious consideration as an early attempt at a difficult task.

Diagnosis in the Classroom

Gill Cotterell

1973

The Centre for the Teaching of Reading, University of Reading

Group; Unstandardized; Any age over seven years; Diagnostic information; Untimed (approximately 15 minutes); Re-usable (only the teachers' booklet is involved); UK.

Diagnosis in the Classroom is a 26-page booklet which discusses the problem of severe backwardness in learning to read and write. It also describes a procedure for screening groups of children using samples of free unaided writing and contains a **Check List of Basic Sounds.** The booklet results from ten years' study of children and adults with specific reading difficulties. It contains reports of observations and provides case-study examples of clinical diagnosis rather than objective criteria.

The author's approach to reading difficulties is based upon examining discrepancies between verbal and non-verbal abilities by using test scores as comparisons. Some factors which show strong links with poor reading abilities, such as language disorders and sequencing difficulties, are discussed.

The diagnostic technique is illustrated with eight examples of children's unaided writing. These are accompanied by further information such as the child's age, reading age, spelling age, and scores for the *Raven's Progressive Matrices* and the *English Picture Vocabulary Test.* Each example is followed by comment, giving a thumbnail sketch of the child.

Thus, diagnosis of difficulty involves careful inspection of the child's writing for content, presentation, use of vocabulary and punctuation. A subjective or clinical diagnosis is then made by considering the child's attainment on standardized tests of verbal and non-verbal ability.

The final section of the booklet gives a two-page Check List of Basic Sounds for diagnosing spelling or reading errors. The sounds on the first of these pages are required for spelling at the eight and a half year level, while the second page lists prefixes, suffixes, more difficult sound units and spelling rules. 'Helpful points for bad spellers' are included on the last page.

Few standard or established techniques exist for the appraisal of language difficulty through written work. This booklet presents a useful prototype approach which merits greater attention and development. In its current form it is probably of only indirect or secondary value to the diagnostician. It is important to note that the guidelines offered in the booklet reflect the author's experience in working with specific learning difficulties or 'dyslexia' and the advice should be evaluated in that context.

Domain Phonic Test and Workshop

J. McLeod and J. Atkinson

1972

Oliver & Boyd

Individual; Unstandardized; Any age; Re-usable Test Cards, Consumable Record Book and Worksheets; Criterion-referenced; Canada.

The Domain test is a criterion-referenced, oral word recognition test, designed to test a comprehensive selection of phonic elements. It includes worksheets for follow-up work. It is particularly suited for use in remedial settings.

The materials consist of four **phonic test cards** (P1-P4), containing rows of test words, a **Record Book** containing an **Auditory Discrimination Test** (P5), 63 **Worksheets** and a **Manual.** The tests are composed as follows:

P1 (48 items) single consonants and vowels
P2 (80 items) single consonants and vowel blends
P3 (69 items) consonant blends, beginning and end; single vowels
P4 (54 items) consonant blends, beginning and end; vowel blends
P5 (50 items) pairs of words are spoken by the teacher, nine are identical, 41 contrast in one phoneme.

Performance on the five tests is noted in the Record Book and summarized in six grids at the back of the book. Worksheets are referenced in each row of the grid. Thus, a child unable to read the initial /st/ in 'stork' (P4) would have this recorded in the third grid (consonant blends) where the teacher is directed to Worksheets 28 and 29 for remedial work. Test P5 is a supplementary test which may alert teachers to a fundamental difficulty in auditory perception. The criterion-referencing principle applies readily to phonic testing and the Domain exemplifies this clearly. The systematic integration of a prepared teaching programme with the tests is a natural extension of criterion referencing. Indeed, this process can be extended using *A Classroom Index of Phonic Resources* by

Doris Herbert and Gareth Davies-Jones (second edition, published by NARE). This crossreferences more published materials and schemes with which the Domain tests can be matched.

Reviews of some other tests have criticized the use of words in isolation. This is less crucial in the case of the Domain, where the focus is upon developing a phonics-based remedial teaching programme rather than measurement of general reading ability. In 1972 when first published in the UK the Domain was a useful advance on current thinking about the testing of reading. Sadly, the rate of progress since then has been slight, particularly beyond the limits of phonics.

Doren Diagnostic Reading Test of Word Recognition Skills

Margaret Doren

1956 (1973 Edition)

NFER-NELSON

Group; Objective; Unstandardized; 6.00–9.00 years; Individual Skill Profile (raw scores); Untimed; One form; Consumable; USA.

The title of this test describes its intention – to diagnose problems in word-attack skills. The test was developed for use with Grades 1–4 in the USA (age range about 6-9 years). The consumable **test booklet** consists of 22 pages of tests and two record sheets. There is also a booklet of 22 **overlay key sheets** for marking.

The test is divided into 12 untimed 'Skill' sections. These are in turn subdivided into component sections arranged in order of difficulty. These skills tests should be spread over several days in order to avoid fatigue, but the number administered at one time is left to the examiner.

The skills included in the test were derived from an analysis of five basic reading programmes in the USA. These skills are sequenced, as far as possible, to reflect a planned development within a reading programme.

Skill 1 'Letter Recognition' (30 items) requires the same letter of the alphabet to be circled within a variety of printed and written styles.

Skill 2 'Beginning Sounds' (25 items) includes the underlining of words to match given pictures and then goes on to sentence completion.

Skill 3 'Whole Word Recognition' (45 items) starts with word matching and goes on to auditory discrimination with the teacher giving relevant words.

Skill 4 'Words Within Words' (30 items) asks for larger words to be split into two smaller ones (e.g. for/get). A further section includes looking for smaller words within larger ones according to auditory precision.

Skill 5 'Speech Consonants' (20 items) measures the ability to identify words read out by the teacher, by choosing one of two.

Skill 6 'Ending Sounds' (35 items) is for the identification of spoken and written words by attending to the final letters. The final section seems largely to be a spelling test of plurals.

Skill 7 'Blending' (20 items) asks for two words to be inserted into each sentence from a set which have identical beginning blends.This exercise seems to focus upon reading and whole word comprehension, rather than blending.

Skill 8 'Rhyming' (40 items) uses both auditory and visual discrimination. In one part of this test the child is asked to use a key by putting 'R' for rhyming words and 'N' for non-rhyming. Other sections ask for odd-one-out words to be deleted.

Skill 9 'Vowels' (90 items) starts with the identification of spoken words which contain certain vowel sounds and goes on to ask for the identification and writing of vowels. This test includes the identification of long and short vowel sounds, and uses irregular spellings and diphthongs.

Skill 10 'Discriminate Guessing' (15 items) measures the ability to supply missing words from clues in the context which consists of riddles and incomplete sentences.

Skill 11 'Spelling' (20 items) has sections of phonetic and non-phonetic words. These are given verbally by the teacher.

Skill 12 'Sight Words' (25 items) measures the ability to read words which do not sound as they are written and to recognize relevant phonetic spellings, e.g. neighbours naebors nigbors negbors.

Results are charted on an individual profile on the cover of the test booklet. This involves simply tabulating the number of wrong responses to each sub-test in the appropriate column. If an error score exceeds seven it will fall in a shaded area and the teacher must look more closely at the child's responses on the sub-test in question. As a crude guide this is probably adequate. However, no explanation is given as to how this takes account of the differences in length and possible differences in difficulty between sub-tests. It may be that the test was so carefully constructed that a score of seven errors places the child at the same point relative to the mean on all the sub-tests. As the **Manual** offers no reassurance on this it would be as well to treat the profile scores with extreme caution and not to attempt any more precise use of results than that outlined in the Manual. A class record sheet, the 'Class Composite', is included with the test. This is used for recording each class member's performance on each component of the 12 skills, indicating areas where practice is required by groups of children.

No information on test reliability is given although a table of generally high correlations of sub-tests with total score is given. This suggests there would be adequate internal consistency. The test was validated by correlation with reading achievements of approximately 40 children in each of Grades 1–4 in four suburban school districts (.77 to .92). Data are also given on the range of scores to be expected at different grade levels and there are norms for 'skill growth' with age. No conversion scales are provided for raw scores.

The Doren differs from some other diagnostic tests of early reading, such as Carver's *Word Recognition Test* (q.v.) or the *Swansea Test of Phonic Skills* (q.v.) by focusing on word-attack skills rather than specific phonic elements. Some teachers might prefer to

approach diagnosis at this level. However, it would seem necessary to have the test administered by an experienced and sensitive teacher, particularly for slower readers. Some of the embodied concepts seem quite advanced (e.g. coding as used in Skills 8 and 9) and could be confusing for some children. Attention must also be given to pronunciation discrepancies by both teacher and pupils. Confusion could occur from dialect differences in those areas which require auditory discrimination. It should also be noted that the test has not been modified for British use and there are references to 'dime', 'hex', and 'platter' which may cause confusion.

The test would be expensive to administer to all children in the ordinary school as the 24-page pupil booklet is consumable. This approach may be useful in specific context in order to provide details for special teaching support.

Durrell Analysis of Reading Difficulty

Donald D. Durrell

1955

NFER-NELSON

Individual; Objective; Standardized; 6.00–12.00; US Grade Equivalents; Untimed (mainly), 30–90 minutes; Re-usable Reading Paragraphs and Tachistoscope, Consumable Record Booklet; USA.

The Durrell Analysis is the more elaborate American prototype on which the better-known *Neale Analysis of Reading Ability* (q.v.) seems to have been based. Like the Neale, it provides norms although the author stresses the diagnostic purpose of the test. The Analysis has seven main parts:

1. Oral Reading Tests. Eight paragraphs of graded difficulty are presented in a ring-bound **Reading Paragraphs booklet.** Norms are based on time taken to read a passage and a record is made of errors and answers to comprehension questions. A checklist is used to note difficulties exhibited.

2. Silent Reading Tests. Eight paragraphs, equal in difficulty to the oral reading paragraphs are used. The child reads a paragraph and recalls as much of the material as possible. A checklist is used to note faulty aspects of performance.

3. Listening Comprehension Tests. Seven paragraphs, one for each US-grade level, with comprehension questions are provided. The selected passages are read out by the tester who then asks the comprehension questions.

The booklet also contains eight supplementary paragraphs, equal in difficulty to the oral and silent reading paragraphs for supplementary testing.

5. Word Recognition and Analysis. This sub-test uses cards of word lists designed to fit into a 'tachistoscope'. This is an elongated envelope with a window which allows successive words on the cards to be exposed for brief periods – ideally at a rate of half a second per word. Word Recognition is tested in this speeded form. If a word is not recognized an untimed exposure is used to assess

'Analysis'. Norms for both tasks are given in the record booklet.

6. Letters. This test involves letter naming, matching (using the tachistoscope) and writing. No norms are used.

7. Visual Memory for Words. Words are displayed in the tachistoscope and the child must identify the word from alternatives printed in the Record Booklet.

8. Sounds. Printed words must be selected to match either the initial, middle or final sound of target words spoken by the tester.

9. Spelling and Handwriting. The spelling test consists of a list of test words presented by the tester in a short sentence. The handwriting test involves copying one of the easier oral reading paragraphs. Grade norms are given for speed of copying.

The **Manual of Directions** contains advice for informal supplementary testing. There are notes on testing the suitability of textbooks for instructions, suggestions for evaluating study abilities, methods of detailed analysis of word abilities and spelling and observed reading interest and effort.

Performance on the tests is recorded on the 12-page **Individual Record Booklet.** The passages in the Reading Paragraphs booklet are reproduced in the Individual Record Booklet in a similar manner to that used in the Neale. Separate grades are recorded for each part of the Analysis and these are represented graphically on a **Profile Chart** in separate bars or columns. This also contains space for results of additional standardized tests of reading and intelligence.

The Manual of Directions describes the rationale of the Analysis and gives procedures for selecting test paragraphs and administering the separate tests. The standardization data are meagre, thereby making difficult the interpretation of normative scores, where these are given. The reliabilities, validities and inter-correlations of the sub-tests are not given. The author claims that wherever norm tables are presented they are based on no fewer than a thousand children for each test and that in the extensive use of these tests the norms have been found to check satisfactorily against other measures of reading ability.

The primary purpose of the Analysis is to discover weaknesses and faulty habits in reading. It is not intended that the Analysis should be used for all children, rather for those who have been selected for individual detailed diagnostic testing as a result of group screening procedures. The author states that the checklists for recording observations of difficulties are the most important feature of the Analysis. 'While norms are provided for many of the tests, a record of the difficulties the child displays is more important than the level of attainment. The items on the checklists are those of the highest frequency and significance in remedial work.'

The main distinction of the test is this great emphasis it places upon detailed observation of the reader and upon alertness to the way in which the various tasks are tackled. Unfortunately, the checklists reflect the reading wisdom of 1955 (and earlier) rather than that

of 1983. Some of the advice offered concerning work on eye movements and eye-voice span reflects now-acknowledged misconceptions of former times. The Analysis can also be criticized for the lack of psychometric rigour and the dubious relevance of its American norms to British children. Also, the reading passages are clearly intended for American readers. No reports are available regarding the extent to which the Durrell Analysis has been used in the UK. Although the test is certainly used in schools in the USA it is hard to believe many teachers in the UK would wish to make serious use of this test.

Early Detection of Reading Difficulties

M.M. Clay

1972 (Second Edition 1979)

Heinemann Educational Books

Individual; Objective; Standardized; 6.00–7.03; Stanine scores; Five sub-tests; Timed, up to 10 minutes each; Most material is chosen from the child's current reading programme; Re-usable; New Zealand.

This 118-page handbook is subtitled 'a diagnostic survey with recovery procedures' and is a greatly extended version of a previous edition. The book contains a programme of activities for diagnosing reading difficulties, advice on 'recovery procedures' for early intervention to prevent reading failure and an account of the research project to evaluate early recovery programmes. It is intended for selective use with children at the time of their sixth birthday if it is considered that they are *not* making good progress with reading at the end of their first year of instruction.

There are four main sub-tests related to reading and three tests related to writing skills are included. The reading sub-tests are as follows:

Record of Reading Behaviour on Books. The teacher makes a 'running record' of the child's reading responses to three texts which are chosen to represent the child's current reading book, a harder text and an easier text. There are detailed guidelines for coding the record, checking directional movement and analysis of errors and self-correction rate.

Letter Identification. The child is asked to respond to all of the letters of the alphabet in both upper and lower case. Responses are analysed for sounding and naming letters, confusions and unknown letters.

Concepts about Print. This test requires the use of one of two specially-printed 20-page reading booklets entitled *Sand* and *Stones*. By working through the booklet with the child according to an exactly-worded format the teacher can examine 24 specific concepts about the printed word. The items cover at least three areas – conventions of print, language of reading instruction and knowledge about punctuation. (Important omissions are knowledge of sentence, paragraph or story and, perhaps, the function of illustrations.) Some concepts are tested by a single item, which raises questions of reliability. The opening instruction to say "I'm going to read you this story but I want you to help me" is unconvincing for most children and some subtler re-wording would be desirable.

Word Tests. There are three equivalent word recognition lists, each of 15 words, taken from the 45 most frequently occurring words in the *Ready to Read* series by the author of these tests. Any alternative words may be used if compiled from the most frequently occurring words in the child's reading material.

The writing test procedures are as follows:

Writing Samples. A number of samples of free writing must be selected and evaluated for 'Language Level', 'Message Quality' and 'Directional Principles' according to criteria specified in the book.

Writing Vocabulary. In this procedure the child is asked to write down 'all the words you know how to write' in ten minutes.

Dictation Test. Five alternate tests, each consisting of two sentences, are available for this test. In scoring, credit is given for every sound written correctly.

Norms for many of the tests – including Writing Vocabulary – are given as 'stanines' (divisions of the normal curve into nine segments) based on research samples of 282 and 320 New Zealand children.

Reliability and validity testing was undertaken with groups of between 40 and 100 children. These were mostly six years old but the age range of 5.00 to 7.00 was included for 'Concepts about Print'. Reliability is quoted as .9 or higher and validity .8 or higher, according to the test. This information is not given in any detail and the statistical work is presented as no more than a subsidiary refinement upon an essentially practical approach to diagnostic assessment.

The *Diagnostic Survey* contains much which should be included in the early stages of teaching a child to read. It could be useful for analysing a school's approach to the prevention of reading failure. However, it is difficult to recommend this particular book, largely because of the confusion in its presentation. The ideas are wrapped up in so much explanation that it takes some time to tease out the essence of the tests themselves. This is a pity as the book contains much which is of potential value. Perhaps its best use would be as a basis for selecting material for in-service study, rather than as a self-contained or free-standing assessment device.

Edwards' Reading Test

Peter Edwards and Ruth Nichols

1980 (UK Edition)

Heinemann

Individual; Unstandardized; 6.00–13.00; Age/Year Levels (related to readability); Untimed (times vary); Consumable Pupil's Record Booklet; UK edition of Australian original.

The Edwards' Test is intended to establish levels of reading material for individual readers on the basis of oral reading accuracy, speed of reading and comprehension/recall.

The core of the test is a series of word-recognition and prose reading tasks presented in a re-usable **Reading Selections booklet.** The main word recognition test, **Edwards' Quick Word Screen Test,** contains eight columns of words, corresponding to age levels between 6.00 and 13.00. A level is mastered if eight or more words are correctly read. A second test, **(Edwards and Sumners' Word List)** contains the '100 most frequent words in English prose materials' and can be used as either a sight vocabulary or spelling test. This may be used if a reader cannot manage the previous test. The major element of the Test is a series of eight oral and eight silent reading passages of 25 to 100 words. These, together with two further passages, can also be used to test listening comprehension. The oral passages are reproduced in a **Pupils' Record Booklet** with the associated comprehension questions, a note of the age level to which each passage corresponds and 'satisfactory' score levels for accuracy, comprehension and speed (in seconds).

Similarly, questions and levels are provided for the eight silent reading passages. The Record Booklet also contains notes on administration and a **Summary Sheet** for recording the dates on which satisfactory performance was reached on each test and passage. Fuller guidelines for administering, scoring and interpreting the Test are presented in a **Manual of Directions.** This also explains, perhaps too briefly, how test results relate to levels of reading material and published lists of books for young and reluctant readers available from Reading University's Centre for the Teaching of Reading.

No evidence for validity or reliability is given. A bibliography of background reading is provided although the sources cited tend to be unpublished research studies or general texts on reading and readability.

Teachers familiar with the concept of readability measurement and 'Informal Reading Inventories' will recognize the underlying theory of the *Edwards' Reading Test* and may well find it a convenient published format for applying these ideas. Basically, a satisfactory score level is taken to show how far the pupil is ready for material of a given reading age, or 'readability' level.

However, the principles the Edwards' Test embodies are essentially part of a do-it-yourself approach to matching readers and texts, and there is no evidence to show that the results obtained using this test are in any way more authoritative than those resulting from teacher-made materials. Nevertheless, the Edwards' Test could provide either an example or foundation upon which both expertise and 'local' materials might be developed.

In general format, the Edwards' Test is similar to the better-known *Neale Analysis of Reading Ability* (q.v.). Indeed, in quality of content and breadth the Edwards' could be regarded as a modest improvement over the Neale although teachers sensitive to sex-role stereotyping would discern distinct bias in some of the Reading Selections passages. Also, the Neale does have the benefit of a conventional standardization (albeit in 1958!) while the Edwards' uses a much more speculative method of age grading seemingly derived from readability research and the authors' intuitive judgements. Some careful thought (together with reference to texts on readability, such as Colin Harrison's *Readability in the Classroom* (Cambridge University Press, 1980) would be merited before becoming committed to use of the *Edwards' Reading Test* on any scale.

Get Reading Right

Stephen Jackson

1971

Robert Gibson, 17 Fitzroy Place, Glasgow, G3 7SF

Group and Individual Sections; Unstandardized; Any Age (Reading Ages below 6.00, up to 9.00); Raw Scores (diagnostic information); Consumable; UK.

These materials would be usable with most age groups requiring remedial phonic help. The materials consist of a **handbook** and **record card** and a set of 11 **Phonic Skills Test Cards**. Tests 1 and 2 are group tests for knowledge of capital and small letters, while the rest are individually administered for checking various phonic skills.

Tests 3 to 11 cover letter sounds, two and three letter words, final consonant blends and 'silent e', initial consonant blends, vowel digraphs and silent letters, word endings and multi-syllabic words. Both teacher and pupil have a copy of the test and the teacher records the child's response to allow for comparison at a later stage.

The tests are untimed and it is not necessary to give all of them, or even the whole of one test, to a pupil. A record card enables details of strengths and weaknesses to be noted together with teaching points. As soon as enough gaps are found to provide focus for teaching, the test can be stopped until a later stage with the same sheet used again to check progress.

No information is included in the manual about the test's development. It seems likely that it was produced in the light of the author's practical experience rather than through a programme of research.

The strength of *Get Reading Right* is in its direct application to the child's needs and the teaching/ learning situation. As soon as the child demonstrates errors which require attention, a programme is devised in order to develop and give practice with specific phonic skills. This leads towards efficient and meaningful use of time and is likely to be motivating for the child. Suggestions for many activities are included in the teachers' handbook, being presented in relation to each test and, like the *Domain Phonic Test* (q.v.), it is crossreferenced in the NARE *Index of Phonic Resources*.

Harrison-Stroud Reading Readiness Profiles

M. Lucile Harrison and James B. Stroud

1950, 1956

NFER-NELSON

Group (one individual section); Objective; Standardized; Beginning Reading – about 6.00; Percentiles; Tests 1–5, one hour thirty minutes (group); Test 6, three minutes (individually); Consumable; USA.

This battery of six sub-tests focuses upon pre-reading skills and its use may presuppose conditions where children will be classified and grouped for early reading instruction at the age of six years. Test material is included in three consumable **booklets** for the pupil but all instructions are contained in the **Teacher's Manual,** which is essential. The front page of Booklet No. 1 serves as an individual record sheet and there is a separate **Class Record Sheet.**

Test 1, Using Symbols (24 items, 15 minutes). The child is asked to draw a line from a word to an appropriate picture.

Test 2, Making Visual Discriminations (32 items, 30 minutes). This test requires the identification of a given word within a line of four others.

Test 3, Using the Context (20 items, 12 minutes). The child must underline one picture from three according to its appropriateness in the context of the teacher's oral instruction, e.g. 'The children saw something with a worm in its mouth flying to a nest. One picture shows what the children saw. Draw a line under it.'

Test 4, Making Auditory Discriminations (18 items, 14 minutes). The child is asked to discriminate between spoken words with similar or different initial consonants.

Test 5, Using Context and Auditory Clues (20 items, 13 minutes). In this test the child's choice is guided by both context and auditory clues, thus combining the tasks in the two previous tests.

Test 6, Giving the Names of the Letters (3 minutes). This includes both capital and lower case forms, printed on a **test card,** which the child is asked to name during a short individual test.

Scores for each test are recorded on a profile chart on the front page of Booklet No. 1 where percentile rankings are given. This gives areas of strengths and weaknesses upon which teaching decisions can be based. Individual scores can be transferred to a class record sheet which also requires IQ and Mental Age scores in order to 'classify' pupils into five types to be grouped together for instruction.

The authors claim 'intrinsic validity' for the tests, but present no statistical evidence for validity or reliability. The standardization upon which the percentile norms are based was carried out with 1,400 American children in 1955.

While this test may be of use in the USA where teaching is more widely based upon test results than in the UK, it seems to require a disproportionate amount of resources for the information it provides. Moreover, it is based upon the assumption that IQ is a strong indicator of learning potential. Such thinking enjoyed greater credibility 35 years ago than currently. It may be worth applying the Profiles where a child seems to be having difficulty in beginning reading but general use as a routine means of grouping children for instruction cannot be recommended.

Infant Reading Tests

Alan Brimer and Bridie Raban

1979

Educational Evaluation Enterprises

Small Group; Objective; Standardized; Infants; Scale Scores (1–7); Untimed (6 tests, 20 minutes each); Consumable; UK.

These tests consist of three **Pre-Reading Tests** and three **Reading Tests** printed in separate booklets. They are intended for diagnostic use during the infant years to identify areas of probable weakness and to monitor maturation and learning during this period.

The Pre-Reading tests use mainly pictorial and symbolic material to examine linguistic, cognitive and perceptual processes identified in research by Professor Brimer into early reading:

> Test 1 (26 items) requires the child to manipulate sentences in which words are represented by simple pictures and symbols. The teacher presents the sentence in its spoken form and the child must identify particular word-equivalent pictures or symbols or complete sentences by selecting appropriate equivalents.
>
> Test 2 (30 items) tests ability to identify middle, beginning and end sounds in words. A target picture is presented and one of four further alternative pictures must be selected which portrays an object which shares an initial, medial or terminal sound in its name with that of the target.
>
> Test 3 (32 items) involves sets of four shapes, letters or words, two of which are identical and must be matched.

The Reading Tests involve word recognition, sentence completion and comprehension:

> Test 1 (24 items) presents sets of four words, unrelated in meaning but with similarities in sound and appearance. The teacher reads out a target word to be selected from the set.
>
> Test 2 (25 items) requires the selection of one of four words to complete a sentence spoken by the teacher.

> Test 3 (22 items) involves selection of one of three sentences which would most appropriately follow a single preceding sentence.

The back page of Test 3 contains space for recording general observations about the child and completion of a simple profile of performance on the tests. The 11-page **Administrative Manual** explains the purpose and rationale of the tests and gives administration instructions and scoring guides. Internal consistency reliability for the tests ranges from .88 to .95. No evidence is given for the validity of the tests beyond a short note on interpretation which states briefly what the tests are measuring. No reference is made to standardization. Raw scores are converted to a seven-point scale based on Rasch analysis or to 'approximate' reading ages between 5.10 and 7.00 for Reading Test 3. The seven-point system is not explained in a way which most teachers could be expected to understand. Essentially, units on the scale are 'equal' in terms of ability level – a score of 6 represents twice the ability of a score of 3 in a way which would not apply to comparison of reading ages 7.00 and 14.00 years, for example. Perhaps the most relevant explanation of this approach to educational test scores is given by Choppin in Chapter 5 of *Assessment and Testing of Reading* (M. Raggett, C. Tutt and P. Raggett, eds., Ward Lock Educational, 1979). Incidentally, the use of Rasch scaling has been criticized in relation to the national programme of Language Monitoring conducted by the Assessment of Performance Unit of the DES. However, it is not clear how far – if at all – the criticisms would apply to tests designed for school use.

It is hard to tell how widely these tests are used but the Pre-Reading tests certainly embody some useful ideas concerning sound-symbol correspondence and left-to-right sequence. However, some informal exploration suggests that children have difficulty in distinguishing between some of the symbols employed in Test 1. Some of the material also proves puzzling to teachers on first examination – the opaque technical notes on the Rasch model do not help, either.

The tests involve a substantial commitment of time and energy on the teacher's part – as the authors acknowledge. It may be that the test materials could best be used on an information and partial basis as an occasional check-up for individual children rather than as a general policy for all children.

Linguistic Awareness in Reading Readiness (LARR) Test

John Downing, Dougas Ayers and Brian Schaefer

1983

NFER-NELSON

Group; Objective; Unstandardized; Beginning of Infant or First School; Raw Scores; Untimed, (45-60 minutes); Equivalent Forms (2); Consumable; Canada.

The LARR Test is intended to measure how far children in the initial stages of schooling have developed concepts and insights into the function, purpose and nature of written language. The authors state that it is useful for determining strengths and weaknesses of both groups and individuals and that it may have diagnostic value with older children. LARR differs from conventional reading readiness tests in that it focuses on linguistic awareness rather than perceptual and cognitive development.

The test is in three parts, printed in separate **test booklets,** each of which takes 15–20 minutes, with recommended breaks or rest periods in between. Each part has two equivalent forms, A and B, but these cannot be used simultaneously as the precise wording of the instructions is not the same for Forms A and B on the second part of the test. The three parts are composed as follows:

Part 1, Recognizing Literacy Behaviour (22 items). A series of pictures are presented in which an object or activity is displayed which is related to reading. The first 11 items require the child to identify things to be read, such as the sign on the side of a bus. The next three items involve identification of a person portrayed in the act of reading. There are then two items in which writing tools must be identified. The final set of items requires identification of people portrayed in the act of writing.

Part 2, Understanding Literacy Functions (23 items). Again, a pictorial identification format is used. In each case a person who is using the written word for a specified activity must be identified – enjoying a story; obtaining information; making public announcements; receiving private messages; telling a story; communicating information; aiding memory; sending a private message; giving directions; leaving a reminder; communication in trade; obtaining information; recording observations; social communication.

Part 3, Technical Language of Literacy (30 items). In this part the child must demonstrate understanding of the concepts of 'Number', 'Letter', 'Printing', 'Writing', 'Line', 'Word', 'Capital Letter', 'Punctuation', 'Letter in Word', 'Sentence' and 'Name'. The items consist of elongated rectangles containing various sets of symbols, words or sentences and the child is instructed to circle a specified feature or component in a way which would demonstrate understanding of the salient linguistic concept. For example, item 16 contains a four-word sentence and the child is instructed to circle the 'first word in the box'.

Every item in LARR has a simple picture printed next to it. Before an item is presented the child is instructed to place a finger on the associated picture. This would ensure that all the children respond to the appropriate item. Although LARR has been classified as an objective test it should be noted that in some places the child is required to circle parts of a picture or to pick out more than one element in the materials presented and this could give rise to some ambiguities. The scoring instructions in the **Administrative Manual** advise that there may be some cases where the teacher must use judgement to evaluate a child's intentions in answering. However, it is also claimed that such instances are rare.

The Manual presents, somewhat briefly, a rationale for the test and refers to the work of cognitive developmental psychologists as well as reading researchers in identifying the importance of concepts about language in early reading. It suggests that LARR would be useful in monitoring the development of these concepts and in evaluating attempts to foster them. Subsequently there is a discussion on the interpretation of LARR results. It is suggested that weakness on Part 1 is indicative of immaturity stemming from lack of relevant background experiences of literacy activities. Part 2 may point to more specific needs to experience real-life uses of written language. Part 3 may alert the teacher to ignorance of the formal features of language which teachers may take for granted but which are entirely novel to many children on first entering school. Four books are recommended which contain 'practical suggestions or descriptions of superior teaching procedures' for further development of the concepts and forms of awareness tested by LARR.

For each part of the test a **Class Evaluation Record** is provided which teachers are advised to use. These require a detailed cross tabulation of each child's performance on each of the 75 items and calculation of individual totals both for pupils and items. This might well allow the teacher to pinpoint major group weaknesses, although the amount of clerical work required would be considerable.

The development of the test appears to have been confined to samples of children in British Columbia. The items were validated in three trials with groups of about 300 children. Whether this is a wholly satisfactory basis for determining the suitability of the test for UK children is debatable. However, the detectable bias towards the experience and cultural background of children in British Columbia in the pictorial content is slight – there is none at all in the spoken directions. The Manual presents internal consistency reliability values for each part and form of the test in the three trials. Some of these were rather low. There were subsequent modifications incorporated into the current published version so that the authors state, 'It is expected that all reliabilities should be above 0.85'. No evidence for the statistical equivalence of the two forms is given or for equivalent form reliability. The validity of the test rests upon content validity – which the authors regard as good – and predictive validity. The latter is based upon the relationship between LARR and performance on a standardized reading test taken a year later amongst children in the first tryout. Unfortunately, the account of results from this study is not always easy to follow. An overall correlation between the reading test and Parts 1 and 3 (Form A) of .50 is given, and for Part 3 (Form B) it is .60. A fuller table of correlations for 12 selected classes is presented. These show considerable variations between classes. Part 3 appears to be consistently the best predictor of later reading attainment while in many classes the other two parts failed to show a statistically significant relationship. However, the numbers in the classes were small and it is questionable that this table is the best way of exploring test validity.

No norms are presented for the test although the Evaluation Record provides space for recording a scaled score (percentile or stanine) 'if class or local district norms are calculated'. The Manual also gives some rough criteria for determining below average scores.

LARR embodies some important ideas about the early development of reading skills. A number of research studies have shown that young children's perception and understanding of the nature and purpose of reading may differ from that of a literate adult. Also, there is a 'technical' language associated with the written word which may be erroneously taken for granted in early reading instruction. This test certainly goes some way in examining how far children had the necessary awareness and understanding to make sense of early reading and the language used by teachers to describe, organize and direct it.

LARR seems to deal with some specific concepts about literacy, yet the authors insist that it is a general measure of conceptual development and that the concepts tested are only 'a sample of the kinds of concepts related to the teaching of reading and writing'. This is confusing. Is LARR to be seen as a criterion-referenced measure focused upon key concepts which are preconditions for successful learning, or is it a global measure of a more general trait which must develop to a certain level? The authors are opposed to the formal teaching of concepts but this does not mean that the test cannot be used to show the teacher whether they have been acquired or not. Also, if the test is to be a more general measure, the absence of some kind of scale or norm system against which to compare progress becomes a severe limitation. There is a third possibility in the diagnostic use of LARR in which performance on the three main parts is compared. The advice on interpreting results refers to this, and the possibility that the parts are not highly intercorrelated, a point noted in the Manual, would make this a fruitful line of development. This would involve the drawing up of a three-part profile for each child and using raw scores, extreme discrepancies might be diagnosed. However, this could probably be done with greater precision if some kind of standardized scaling system was available.

The authors mention that further studies involving LARR are to be carried out and it is to be hoped that these will include some consideration of the three possibilities outlined above. In the meantime, it is to be hoped teachers will make exploratory use of LARR.

Macmillan Diagnostic Reading Pack

Ted Ames

1980

Macmillan Education

Individual; Unstandardized; Untimed; For Children with Reading Ages 6.00–9.00; Re-usable Tests; Consumable Checklists; UK.

The Teacher's Manual for the Macmillan Pack is entitled *Teach Yourself to Diagnose Reading Problems*. This fairly conveys the main intention underlying the materials. The author's experience of in-service work at the John Taylor Teacher's Centre, Leeds, revealed a need for a structured and comprehensive system of diagnostic assessment that would also enable teachers to train themselves in the diagnostic teaching of reading. The Pack is thus, simultaneously, a diagnostic testing system and a vehicle for extending professional skills. The author strongly believes that one cannot structure a reading programme without appraising reading progress as an integral part of the teaching. The Pack is offered as a possible means for doing this.

The published materials consist of the **Teacher's Manual, Checklists** to cover four stages of testing and 13 **test cards.** The central principle of the Pack is the use of four flow charts. These take the teacher through a series of testing and teaching activities. Thus, use of the materials involves a long-term approach to teaching rather than a set-piece, once-and-for-all testing session.

The procedure starts with finding a child's reading age using one of five recommended standardized tests. However, one of those suggested *NFER Reading Test AD* (q.v.) does not actually give a reading age directly. According to the level of reading age one of the four flow-charted reading and teaching procedures is then initiated. Each chart consists of a number of connected 'decision boxes' which represent points for testing. There are 28 tests in all and some of them appear in more than one chart. The author also suggests that with ingenuity many of them can be presented in group form. In addition to the 13 Test

Cards, the tests include standard procedures to be carried out by the teacher, which are described in the appropriate Checklist. The Checklist is also used to record individual test performance.

The Stage 1 flow chart (reading ages 5.00–6.00) deals with initial skills such as letter recognition, auditory and visual processes and simple blending. It culminates in a test for Phonic Readiness. Stage 2 (reading ages 6.00–7.00) covers sight vocabulary of key words, blending, spelling of phonically regular words and higher level skills of comprehension. Stages 3 and 4 (reading ages 7.00–8.00, 8.00–9.00) cover progressively more advanced phonic and word-attack skills and repeat the higher level skills test of Stage 2. The Manual gives scoring instructions for each test and the Checklists give conversion tables which allow raw scores to be scaled out of ten and transferred to an individual **Reading Profile Graph.** This, together with the advice given in the flow charts is designed to allow individual reading programmes to be planned. The Teacher's Manual cross references each test with lists of materials, teaching aids and major texts on teaching reading which discuss the skills under consideration.

The tests and procedures used in the pack are all at the level of 'surface diagnosis' – they directly deal with reading skills rather than underlying psychological causes of backwardness. The author does point out, however, that, while the tests are relevant to the needs of the vast majority of children, there may be exceptional cases where more specialized forms of diagnosis may be needed.

The materials were developed along practical rather than experimental lines and no real evidence for conventional validity or reliability is offered. Reference is made to a correlation of .88 between performance on the three spelling tests used in the Pack and a blending test, presumably based on the same words as the spelling test. Unfortunately, the author's interpretation of the result is slightly misleading. Perhaps more interesting is the reference to positive experience of teachers who have used the diagnostic programme – a form of validation which many more tests of assessment procedures should undergo.

The general composition of the tests reflects much standard practice and belief in the teaching of reading, particularly at the earlier stages. The claim to be *more* comprehensive than other assessment materials is perhaps a little over-stated although there is no doubt that few exceed the Macmillan Pack in this respect. The tests concerned with higher level skills (strategies, use of context, rate and comprehension) are perhaps somewhat thinner and vaguer than the other tests.

Some teachers may baulk at the prospect of a flow chart of assessment and teaching which assumes, or imposes, a uniform pattern of learning for all children. The development of such flow charts certainly assumes a hierarchy or progression of learning which seems arbitrary at times. Nevertheless, close examination of the flow charts reveals no major grounds for disputing the sequences adopted. Any dangers of being overmechanistic would seem slight in compari-

son to the advantages of being exhaustive and orderly.

The Macmillan Pack is a major contribution to the integration of assessment and teaching. Although not all teachers may be temperamentally attuned to the strategy adopted by Ted Ames in these materials it is one which deserves serious consideration in schools, particularly where teachers are less experienced in diagnostic work. The pattern is one which also might be worth exploring more fully in relation to the development of silent reading and more advanced study skills.

Marianne Frostig Developmental Test of Visual Perception (DTVP)

Marianne Frostig

1963

NFER-NELSON

Group or Individual; Standardized; 3.00–10.00; 35–45 minutes; Perceptual Ages and Quotients; Consumable; USA.

The DTVP is designed to measure certain perceptual functions, and to check they are present at the age at which they normally develop. On this basis, it is suggested school success can be predicted in so far as it depends on visual perceptual abilities. Following the identification of children who deviate from the norm, training procedures designed to correct the specific disabilities can then be instigated.

The test items measure a child's performance on a variety of motor tasks against the norms for his age. These tests were chosen because of their seeming relevance to school performance.

1. Eye-Motor Coordination, (16 items). This tests eye/hand coordination and involves the drawing of continuous straight, curved or angled lines between boundaries of various width, or from point to point without guidelines.

2. Figure-Ground, (8 items). This requires the child to select some regular geometric shapes from increasingly complex backgrounds.

3. Constancy of Shape (4 items) . The tasks require recognition of certain geometric figures presented in a variety of sizes, shadings, textures and positions in space, and their discrimination from similar geometric figures. Circles, squares, rectangles, ellipses and parallelograms are used.

4. Position in Space, (8 items). This test involves the discrimination of reversals and rotations of figures presented in series. Schematic drawings representing common objects are used.

5. Spatial relationships, (8 items). Analysis of simple forms and patterns is tested. These items consist of lines of various lengths and angles which the child is required to copy, using dots as guide points.

Performance on the test is recorded on the **profile sheet** which is part of the pupil's **test booklet.** This contains spaces for a Perceptual Age – analogous to reading age – and Perceptual Quotient (age adjusted score).

A 40-page **Administration and Scoring Manual** describes both general and verbatim instructions for administering and scoring the test, including illustrations, and tables for computing all available scores and indices. The 1966 revision of the Manual is to be used in conjunction with a monograph containing the 1963 standardization of the test and some comments on the implications of perceptual development for school performance.

Standardization was carried out by testing over 2,100 children within the age range 3.00–9.00 years. The Manual provides test-retest and split-half reliability coefficients and a variety of correlation coefficients relating the DTVP to reading in the first grade, intelligence, and classroom adjustment.

The test claims to measure five important but relatively unrelated aspects of visual perception. However, many of the sub-tests also require fine motor skills and the conclusions regarding perceptual difficulties must be drawn very carefully. There is inadequate evidence that the DTVP has the diagnostic ability to measure five separate visual perception skills. The majority of studies suggest that it measures just one general visual perception factor.

Interest in the relationship between visual perceptual abilities and reading has been investigated during the past 50 years. Researchers are in agreement that the reading process involves some perceptual skills. However, general agreement is not evident as to the type of perceptual skill nor the degree of relationship between a specific skill and its role in reading performance.

Recent attention has been given to the Frostig 'Programme', designed to assist in strengthening those weaknesses revealed by the test. Whether the training programme is effective because it is similar to the various tests on the DTVP is still being investigated. Earlier claims, that after identification of visual perceptual weaknesses and strengths followed by appropriate training on the Frostig Programme, improvements in visual perception and reading attainments occurred, have not been substantiated.

One could raise the question, 'Of what value to reading is the ability to draw a line from left to right between two lines without touching the borders?'

Pre-Reading Screening Procedures

Beth H. Slingerland

1977

Test Agency

Group; Objective; Unstandardized; 5.00–6.00 approximately); High-Low Rating Scale; Timed sub-tests to be given over 3 sessions; Consumable; USA.

This is the first of a series of diagnostic tests which are imported from the US. The purpose of the *Pre-Reading Screening Procedures* is to find, among children of average to superior intelligence, the ones who show difficulties in auditory, visual and/or kinaesthetic modalities. The author suggests that a child with an inadequate performance may have a specific language disability and will need extra instruction in order to prevent early failure in reading, writing, spelling and verbalization skills.

The pencil and paper tasks are contained within a 15-page **pupil booklet.** Twelve separate procedures, administered in three sittings, assess aspects of visual and auditory perception, and combinations of these with kinaesthetic motor skills. A separate task requires the pupil to repeat words spoken by the tester. A separate four-page **record sheet** includes a teacher observation schedule and provision for summarizing areas of identified difficulty. The 90-page **Manual** gives clear administration and interpretation instructions.

Many of the tasks employed in the Slingerland will be familiar to teachers who are acquainted with the better-known diagnostic tests of UK origin. It is unlikely that many teachers would need to make routine use of this test. However, some of the evaluation procedures may be worth consulting by practitioners as a basis for extending their own approach to diagnosis.

Reading Diagnostic Tests

Arthur Gates, Anne McKillop and
Elizabeth Horowitz

1981

Test Agency

Individual; Objective; Standardized; 6.07–12.02;
Grade Equivalents; Untimed; Re-usable Test Materials, Consumable Pupil Record Booklet; USA.

The object of this battery of individual tests is to gain detailed diagnostic information of a child's reading, writing and spelling skills. Specific sub-tests in reading involve oral accuracy and fluency, sight recognition, blending ability, phonic knowledge, auditory blending and discrimination, spelling and writing. American grade norms are given but the primary objective is to examine the performance of individual children.

The test materials are presented in a **ring-bound booklet.** The initial oral reading test (which is not illustrated) has seven paragraphs in ascending order of complexity which build up into a single story. There are no oral comprehension checks, though the tester could informally include these. The remainder of the sub-tests are selected as considered necessary following the pupil's oral reading.

A sentence reading test is followed by two consecutive tests of 40 words presented first by flashing (tachistoscopically*) and secondly allowing the pupil unlimited time for decoding. Following this are three word-attack tests – syllabication, recognizing and blending of word parts and reading short words. In all cases 'nonsense' words are used in order that no 'sight recognition' factor is introduced. Pupils then may be directed to sub-tests involving knowledge of letter names and sounds if considered necessary. Two auditory tests – one of auditory blending and one of discrimination – are included and a thirty-word graded spelling test and an informal writing sample complete the battery. (The latter of course has no norms given in the administration manual.) A 12-page **Pupil Record Booklet** is used to record performance on each test and for the pupil to perform the two final written tasks.

The test was first published in 1962 as the *Gates-*

McKillop Reading Diagnostic Tests. Although popular in the USA this test was not widely available in the UK. There are few changes in the 1981 edition but a new standardization on 600 American children from ten

* See the entry for the **Durrell Analysis of Reading Difficulty.**

schools was done. A test-retest study of 27 children gave a correlation of .94 and correlations with reading attainments test scores from .68 to .96 are reported. Comparisons were made with the previous 1962 version of the test: 2nd grade levels were significantly different in grades 1–4 (ages 6.00–9.02) but very similar for older children. Assistance is given in the manual for conversion to ages, but no British sampling has been done. The size and quality of the American sampling do not inspire confidence in the 'reading ages', but since the essential information is diagnostic teachers may not find this a problem.

The whole battery would take over an hour for each pupil. In most cases it takes 45 minutes to achieve a diagnostic profile. Information gained from comparing flashed and untimed scores on 40 words may be of interest but there is too much emphasis on nonsense words in all the phonic subtests.

Indeed, the entire test is lamentably devoid of meaning for the child. Even the 'story' passages for oral reading excite little interest from children. Since accurate 'barking at print' is all that is essentially required by the exercise it has to be said that the test does not test 'reading' as we understand it in contemporary usage. Some of the later passages are so contrived it is positively embarrassing to present them to children. The style is bizarre and bears little relation to modern prose:

'stop irritating me and my noble rodent kinsmen and mayhap we shall permit thee the privilege of sojourning briefly in these our exclusive provinces . . .'

The detailed nature of the sub-tests suggests the process of reading is a separate series of simply-related sub-skills. It was this 'atomistic' approach to reading that led to the phonic purges of the 1950s and left many stunted but 'accurate' readers cold at the prospect of processing ever more banal meaningless primers until they vowed never to read again.

Having said that, it is still essential to evaluate technical performance so that remedial strategies can be designed to fulfil the needs of individuals. There is some virtue, therefore, in having the sub-tests organized in one battery rather than several. Whilst this is not particularly inspiring or up-to-date, it cannot be criticized for lack of thoroughness except in the area of comprehension. Unfortunately it represents an approach to reading belonging more to the archives of the teaching of reading than to contemporary diagnostic procedures.

Reading Level Tests (Experimental Version)

National Foundation for Educational Research

1974

NFER-NELSON

Group or Individual; Objective; Unstandardized; 7.00–10.00; Fry's Readability level (adapted); Untimed – approximately 10–15 minutes; Consumable; UK.

The *Reading Level Tests* are intended for use in conjunction with other measures to assess the comprehension of prose material graded for readability. They may be used for the assessment of reading development and subsequent selection of suitable reading material for pupils.

The tests consist of eight cloze passages issued in two **test booklets.** Part 1 is intended for first and second year juniors, Part 2 for third and fourth year pupils. Each booklet contains four passages.

Raw scores are converted to express a corresponding readability level, as estimated from Fry's Readability Chart. The scores aim to indicate the levels of text that a child might be able to deal with for either independent or instructional reading purposes. The test is thus an indirect measure of the reading age of reading material to which a child is suited.

The ten-page **Manual** contains an introduction, rationale, details of construction, administration and marking, interpretation (tabular representations) of the passages with reference to the three levels, an appendix with instructions for the use of Fry's Readability Chart, and bibliography (nine references).

Correlations between Fry's dimensions of syllable and sentence length, and mean score on cloze passages with a sample of 740 junior school children, are between 0.7 and 0.8. Internal reliability is high ($KR20 = 0.96$).

Throughout the Manual for these tests, it is emphasized that they are experimental and thus should be used as a supplementary guide for the teacher rather than for norm-referenced assessment. With this disclaimer having been made, the attempt to provide a fairly swift method of assessing a child's level of reading comprehension in context is to be welcomed. However, it is important to realize that the concepts of readability and comprehension and their assessment through the use of cloze procedure tests such as these remain problematic (Hewett, 1982). Similarly, the meaning of the statistics derived from the partial standardization is open to question. Nevertheless, if, as suggested in the Manual, teachers acquaint themselves with the notions of cloze procedure and readability, it may well be that they could devise their own classroom-based measures which would prove more directly relevant to the work of pupils than the passages used in the tests, and be of greater use to the teacher in the assessment of comprehension. A brief note of cloze procedure is given in Appendix A and Robertson (1981) reviews the most important findings in the area of cloze procedure. The three levels of readability outlined would also seem to be of more use when related to specific classroom material. This is not possible in a test designed for general use.

References
HEWITT, G. (1982). 'A Critique of Research Methods in the Study of Reading Comprehension,' *British Educational Research Journal*, 8, 1, pp. 9-21.
ROBERTSON, C.G. (1981). 'Cloze Procedure: A Review,' *Educational Research, 23, 2, pp. 128-33*.

Reading Miscues Inventory

Yetta Goodman and Caroline Burke

1972

Macmillan USA, New York

Individual; Unstandardized; Any age; Untimed; USA.

The *Reading Miscues Inventory* (RMI) provides a way to analyse the errors or 'miscues' a reader makes when reading aloud from a text. This careful analysis indicates the reading strategies children use as well as their strengths and weaknesses.

The authors argue that any deviations from the expected response (i.e. what is on the printed page) are not random. Rather, the deviation, or miscue, reflects the reader's own use and experience of language. The reader predicts which word is likely to come next using knowledge of the grammar (syntax) and the meaning (semantics). For example, Goodman and Burke suggest that any English speakers faced with "The _ _ _ was chewing on a bone" knows that only a limited number of words will fit. Nouns such as 'dog', 'cat' and 'lion' are likely possibilities but words such as 'yellow', 'happen', and 'quickly' will not usually be tried. By examining the miscues, it is possible to identify the predominant method(s) and strategies being used by the reader and thereafter to extend the reader's repertoire of possible strategies. To quote from the RMI Handbook:

'Given the test "The duck walked under the old apple tree"
Sandy reads "The duck walked under the apple tree"
Robin reads "The duck walked under the old apple three"

Sandy omits 'old' which does not alter the meaning substantially, whereas Robin does not seem aware of the meaninglessness of his reading. On a standardized test, Robin and Sandy would be penalized equally although their problems are quite different.'

The full RMI enables a teacher to make a detailed examination of the miscues made by a pupil as he records an unfamiliar text or audio tape. The pupil is also required to retell the story in his own words with sufficient prompts by the teacher to recall as many details of plot, character and descriptions as possible. The text should be sufficiently difficult for about 25 miscues to be made but not so difficult that the pupil will be unable to continue independently.

Marking is organized around five basic kinds of miscues: substitution; omission; insertion; reversal; repetition. With the help of a standard coding sheet, the teacher can create a RMI profile of strengths and weaknesses of the reader with a view to providing an appropriate reading programme for the pupil. The profile has bar graphs related to Comprehension, Grammatical Relationships, Sound/Graphic relationships and the Retelling score. For each of these, there are specifically linked strategy lessons in the Handbook where the implications of the weakness are described in more detail alongside the general principles behind the strategies. Equipped with this information, any teacher would be able to plan appropriate reading activities for that child.

The RMI kit includes a 133-page **Handbook, Reader Profile Sheets, Practice Analysis Tapes, Practice Analysis Manual, Coding Sheets for Diagnosis and Evaluation** and **Worksheets of Readings** set out with numbered lines for easy coding.

The Handbook is really a summary of classroom implementations of Kenneth and Yetta Goodman's 'psycholinguistic' theory and is unequivocal in approach. Thus, teachers are warned against imposing isolated drill practices for readers who consistently make graphic/sound confusions. Rather, the reader must have a supportive language context to find out for himself the relationship between the sound and corresponding written symbol. Many teachers might find this both too prescriptive and unrealistic especially if they have found that phonic methods contribute substantially to fluent reading.

There are practical difficulties in applying the published RMI in the way prescribed. It would be necessary to set aside 15–20 minutes to hear the child read and record miscues on the worksheet. It would also be essential to obtain an audible recording. However, Elizabeth Goodacre has suggested a simpler form of analysis in *Hearing Children Read* (Centre for the Teaching of Reading, Reading University, 1981) which is also much more directly accessible to British teachers.

Nevertheless, the RMI is an important contribution

to reading assessment. One of the most important aspects of miscue analysis is the way it demonstrates that not all oral reading errors are equally serious – some indicate the partial development of intelligent reading strategies. A revision to be published shortly may be less complex and more attractive for regular classroom use. It is to be hoped that it may become more easily available to teachers in the UK.

Slingerland Screening Tests for Identifying Children with Specific Language Disabilities

Beth H. Slingerland

1970

Test Agency

Group, (Individual Auditory Test); Unstandardized; 6.00–12.00; Untimed (approximately 60 minutes); Raw Scores; Consumable; USA.

The first in this series of four self-contained tests was published in 1962. Their purpose is to find those children of normal to superior intelligence in need of specific help in reading or spelling, writing and written expression. In the **Manuals** the test aims are set out as 'the identification of relative strengths and weaknesses in perceptual-motor functions, visual, auditory and kinaesthetic, and to reveal deficits that may exist in one or more of these areas of receptive and expressive language performance'.

The four sets of tests are for use with children in the age range six to twelve years. The forms of the tests differ from each other only in vocabulary difficulty; otherwise, they are the same for all grades in the essential perceptual-motor tasks.

Each of the first three sets contains nine sub-tests. Eight are designed for group administration, and one is for individual testing. The fourth set of tests contains one extra group test:

Tests 1 and 2 require the child to copy models – with ample time for reference – one at a far point and one at a near point. In the first sub-test the children copy from a wallchart, and in the second from a page close at hand.

Test 3 involves the visual perception of words, letters and numbers seen in a brief exposure, one at a time on a card.

Test 4 requires the visual perception of symbols and sequences within words and the ability to perceive similarities and differences.

Test 5 tests the child, with no model before him, to discover whether he has a 'kinaesthetic' as well as a 'visual' memory of what he has perceived.

Test 6 links auditory perception and memory with a visual-kinaesthetic motor association. Groups of letters, numbers and words are dictated and have to be written on the test pages after a brief period of distraction and delay.

Test 7 also tests the auditory-visual-kinaesthetic linkage but adds the requirement of making an auditory discrimination of single sounds within the sequence of sounds in whole words.

Test 8 assesses auditory-visual linkage without the kinaesthetic-motor requirement of writing. Dictation of a word, letter or number group is followed by a brief distraction and delay before it is located among a group printed on the test page.

Test 9 (fourth set only) tests possible confusion in general orientation and laterality as it relates to the self and also the ability to give an idea the desired expression in writing – something that presents no difficulty for non-specific language disability children by the time they reach the sixth or seventh year of schooling.

In the Individual Auditory Test words and phrases spoken by the examiner are echoed by the child, sentences are completed orally, and the child is asked to retell a brief story immediately after he has heard it.

Scoring of performance involves a substantial element of judgement by the teacher and the tests cannot be fairly described as objective. Once scored, performance on the test is initially recorded by completing page two of the pupil's booklet. As a result of this 'Quick Analysis' the teacher makes a decision whether to transfer the scores to a 'Detailed Analysis' section of the pupil's booklet. An evaluation is carried out on the basis of the Detailed Analysis.

A 150-page Manual describes the rationale behind the first three sets of tests; there is a separate 100-page Manual for the fourth set.

The author explains that no attempt has been made to develop 'standardized' norms. It is suggested that the most useful set of norms would be those which are developed in an individual school as the tests are used over a period of time.

Although the Manual has no data on reliability and validity, a **separate pamphlet** on these is provided. It includes results of 'inter-rater' agreement studies which could be interpreted to show that even trained raters differ substantially in marking the same test results. Significant correlations with tests of attainment are reported but a full account of the validation of the Tests is reserved for a **Technical Manual** (not available for this review) obtainable from the American publishers.

It should be emphasized that the tests were designed for use with intelligent children identified as having marginal or extreme specific language disability. They are unlikely to appeal, or be of any practical value, to the majority of teachers although they may have a special interest to practitioners who feel it is relevant to think in terms of specific disorders. However, no information is readily available on the extent, if any, to which the tests have been used in the UK since they were first published in the USA in 1962. Perhaps their main interest is as historical examples of an ultra-diagnostic approach to learning difficulties which, while not necessarily unsound, placed considerable weight on the concept of 'specific' difficulty and made heavy (perhaps excessive) use of diagnostic testing.

Specific Language Disability Test

Neva Malcomensius

1967

Test Agency

Group; Partly Objective; Unstandardized; 12.00–14.00; Raw Scores; Consumable; Timed (varies according to age level); USA.

This test is designed as an extension of the procedures used in Slingerland's *Screening Tests for Identifying Children with Specific Language Disabilities* (q.v.) to the secondary age range.

There are ten sub-tests. Specified time allowances decrease for each test at successive age/US grade levels:

Tests I and II, Visual to Motor, involve copying printed material presented both at a distance and close up.

Test III, Visual Discrimination (6 items), uses a multiple-choice target word selection format. Sets of five alternative spellings of a word are presented and the correct spelling must be identified.

Test IV, Visual Memory (17 items), requires the pupil to recall and identify words and letter and number strings which are flash-presented.

Test V, Visual Memory to Motor (12 items), requires the pupil to copy out some abstract symbols, words and numerical stimuli from memory.

Test VI, Auditory Discrimination (12 items), uses pairs of words dictated by the tester which the pupil must identify as 'same' or 'different'.

Test VII, Auditory Memory to Motor (14 items), is a dictation test using short phrases and numerical material.

Test VIII, Auditory to Visual (12 items), is a multiple-choice test in which words or numbers spoken by the tester must be selected from alternatives printed in the test booklet.

Test IX, Comprehension, requires the pupil to write out from memory a paragraph read aloud by the tester.

Test X, Spelling – Auditory to Motor (20 items), is an orally-presented spelling test.

Pupils write their answers in a **test booklet** although some of the test materials are presented on separate **display cards** and **charts.** These do not appear to be available from the British distributor, but adequate instructions are given for teachers to make their own materials. The number of Omissions, Errors, Self-corrections and Reversals in pupils' answers are recorded on a grid in the answer booklet and the administration instructions include some notes on 'evaluating' the response to each test.

No technical information of any sort is given. The Manual provides no information on the rationale underpinning the tests except for an acknowledgement to Beth Slingerland for allowing the author to extend her tests to junior high school level.

Some of the sub-tests may be of value in identifying severe – and rare – cases of dysfunctioning amongst secondary-aged pupils, but even this is to stretch plausibility to an extreme. It is hard to see any real value for this test. Indeed, although the alleged dangers of testing are sometimes over-estimated this seems to be a case where positive harm *could* be done if the author's absurd claim that 'it is generally accepted that approximately twenty out of every hundred students have some degree of dyslexia' were taken seriously. (It is also advised that 'a few will have such severe learning difficulties that class learning is impossible. Private tutors should be secured for such students.')

Standard Achievement Recording System
(STARS) (in *A Technology of Reading and Writing Volume 2: Criterion-Referenced Tests for Reading and Writing*)

Judith M. Smith, Donald E.P. Smith and James R. Brink

1977

Academic Press Inc. (London)

Group and Individual; Objective (some); Unstandardized; Consumable; USA.

Recommended uses for STARS range from classroom diagnosis of individual pupils to assessment of 'classroom productivity' in schools or across groups of schools. The authors suggest that some 'proper and productive' ways of using STARS 'have yet to be invented'.

STARS is based on a comprehensive model of reading and writing skills covering the general primary age range. It is composed of 48 test 'series' individually containing as many as 21 sub-tests which may themselves have between three and 20 items each. The tests themselves are not marketed in the UK but a complete sample set, together with a discussion of the system on which they are based, can be found in *A Technology of Reading and Writing Volume 2*.

STARS was developed in Michigan and some of the main intended uses are on a scale incompatible with the resources or inclinations of most British schools. It has been included for review in this volume as a highly developed example of the US approach to criterion-referenced testing and because the complete test system can be examined in a book which is available in Britain.

The tests are organized to reflect an ascending hierarchy of skills in written language:

Level	Sub-test Series	No. of Tests
Letter Skills	Shapes	8
	Manuscript Form	14
	Cursive Form	11
	Names	8
	Letter-Sound Equivalents	12
	Functions	6

Level	Sub-test Series	No. of Tests
Word Skills	Shapes	5
	Phonology	18
	Word Recognition	11
	Spelling	5
	Vocabulary: Syntactic	13
	Vocabulary: Semantic	9
	Vocabulary: Classification	12
	Vocabulary: Fluency	7
Sentence Skills	Oral Reading	3
	Space Between Words	1
	Sentence Memory	2
	Dictation	6
	Capitalization	10
	Punctuation	21
	Transformations	17
	Directions	2
	Questions	6
	Sentence Meaning	3
	Figurative Language	4
Paragraph Skills	Form Convention	2
	Grammatical Patterns	4
	Phonological Patterns	5
	Universe of Discourse	2
	Topic	5
	Plot	8
	Referential Links	2
	Relational Links	6
	Information	9
	Summarisation	5
	Induction	6
	Deduction	3
	Focus	5
	Point of View	4
	Mood	3
	Oral Reading	4
Book Skills	Fiction	7
	Non-fiction	5
	Textbooks	7
	Reference Works	9
	Periodicals	3
	Letters	6

Some of the tests require the teacher to judge the correctness of pupils' responses, others are more objective. A test is only considered 'mastered' when all items are correctly answered.

Much of the explanatory text in the book is devoted to discussing the problems of validating STARS. It constitutes a useful discussion of general problems in validating criterion-referenced tests although the style of the book is often tortuous – inattentive children are referred to as having 'attentional deficits'. Three criteria of validity are proposed: 'task analytic'; 'psychometric'; 'systemic'. By 'task analytic' validity the authors seem to mean that the tests present an acceptable breakdown or specification of the tasks faced in learning to read and write. 'Content validity' and 'face validity' are perhaps more familiar terms for this. A detailed account of the processes tested is presented and ultimately validity in this sense rests upon the judgement of individual readers. 'Psychometric' validity subsumes the conventional reliability and validity criteria described in the Introduction to this book. KR20 values for the 18 Phonology tests are presented and range from .38 (low) to .88 (moderate). Correlations between STARS and standardized achievement tests are also cited. These are low and are based on small numbers of testees. In addition data are tabulated displaying proportions of pupils mastering various tests in field trials. As proof of validity this is questionable. The discussion of 'systemic' validity suffers from even greater confusion. We learn this is the 'capacity of an instrument to become a contributing part of the instructional ecosystem' – the practical impact of the tests in schools. The limited first-hand evidence for this in the case of STARS is alarming, being based upon the 'backwash' effect created when STARS was introduced into certain Michigan schools! Generally the book contains more discussion of validity than convincing proof of it.

STARS exemplifies a fundamental problem in criterion-referenced assessment of language skills. Criterion-referencing requires a degree of explicitness about what is to be learned which can lead to fragmentation and trivialization. STARS approaches language as a taught subject like history or mathematics. Thus all the test items involve either 'recognition' or 'reproduction' of highly particularized points of learning. Some teachers may welcome such a structured approach, certainly the analysis provided by Smith *et al.* is not too distant from that any thoughtful teacher might make, given unlimited time to do so. Others may feel that by breaking language teaching into constituent parts STARS ceases to be about language at all. Certainly, STARS confuses an analysis of what, in a formal sense, has to be learned with how it is learned. Above all, the scheme loses sight of language as an essentially *communicative* activity.

Standard Reading Tests

> **J.C. Daniels and Hunter Diack**
>
> **1958 (Thirteenth impression 1977)**
>
> **Hart-Davis Educational**

Individual (one group); Objective; Partly Standardized; 5.00–14.00; Reading Ages and Reading Standards; Untimed; Re-usable; UK.

This is a battery of tests, published in book form, which seems to be widely used and popular with many teachers. They are intended to give detailed information upon which a relevant teaching programme can be built. The content includes many aspects of the reading process such as visual and aural discrimination, letter and word recognition, silent reading, comprehension and spelling.

The two most widely used tests, from the battery of 12, have also been published separately. Test 1, the Standard Test of Reading Skill, is available as a set of **individual cards** for each of the 36 items. Test 12 (referred to in the book as Test 12 Graded Test of Reading Experience) is available on three sheets of **spirit duplicating masters.**

These present the 50 sentences of Test 12 in graded print, thus making a better relationship to reading levels. Instructions and interpretations for all tests are given in the book only, so these separate publications are supplementary and could not stand on their own.

The tests are as follows:

Test 1, The Standard Test of Reading Skill (Individual). This is an individual test which can be used at six-monthly intervals to monitor reading progress up to a reading age of nine years. It is a series of 36 sentences in question form which the child reads aloud and then gives a considered answer to the teacher. However, it is the reading of the question which is assessed, leaving the answering of the questions to be undertaken in a relaxed manner with the teacher able to discuss possibilities with the child. A table of reading ages is given from five to nine years.

If a child's reading performance on Test 1 causes concern, one or more of the following diagnostic tests may be used.

Test 2, Copying Abstract Figures (Individual). This is for children with a reading age of less than 5.03 years, for children with poor eye/hand coordination or difficulty in left/right orientation. As the heading suggests, there are four abstract figures to be copied. Results are appraised for Accuracy and 'Neatness'.

Test 3, Copying a Sentence (Individual). In copying a sentence the child illustrates awareness of word units as well as the motor skills required for writing. It is for pupils who have a reading age below 5.06 years and who are guessing from parts of words in Test 1.

Test 4, Visual Discrimination and Orientation (Individual). A series of pictures, shapes or groups of letters are matched from a group of four. This test is used for further demonstration of left/right or mirror-image confusion.

Test 5, Letter Recognition (Individual). This demonstrates the child's knowledge of alphabetic names, phonic sounds, initial consonants and final consonants in words. It is to be used with children who have no grasp of letter sounds and give wrong sound values in Test 1.

Test 6, Aural Discrimination (Individual). To test for partial or pseudo-deafness by asking the child to choose an appropriate picture in relation to a given sound.

Test 7, Diagnostic Word-Recognition (Individual). There are eight sub-tests in this section, each consists of a word list focusing upon specific functions:

a. Phonically simple two and three letter words.
b. Consonantal blends at beginning of phonically simple words.
c. Consonantal blends at ends of words.
d. Polysyllabic phonically simple words.
e. Graded phonically complex words.
f. Common words with irregular spellings.
g. 'Reversible' words.
h. Nonsense syllables.

The child reads the sub-test while the teacher notes words which are missed or erroneously read.

Test 8, Oral Word-Recognition (Individual). The child is told a word by the teacher and asked to point to the correct written version from a choice of four. This test is intended to use with children who read using minimal clues and guessing, for those who have difficulties in picking out sounds or who confuse pairs of letters.

Test 9, Picture Word-Recognition (Individual) – to be given with Test 8. In this test, the child is asked to choose from a line of four words to match a picture. It is for children who read aloud without comprehension or who guess words from the context. (Such a strategy is no longer considered to be necessarily a sign of faulty reading.)

Test 10, Silent Prose-Reading and Comprehension (Individual). Children with a reading age of about eight years but whose independent reading appears below this level may be tested for understanding of continuous prose by answering the questions provided.

Test 11, Graded Spelling (Individual or Group). A table of norms to give a spelling age (from 5.00 to 12.03 years) is provided with this test. It is for any child or group of children for whom a spelling test is considered to be necessary.

Test 12, Graded Test of Reading Experience (Group). This test is for children with a reading age of 7.05 years or more who may be entrenched in a mechanical approach to reading at the expense of comprehension. Fifty sentences are given – a copy should be made for each child. Each sentence is completed by underlining one word from a choice of four. A table of norms gives reading ages from 6.00 to 14.00+ years, but the user is warned that reading ages about 10.00 years are unreliable and misleading. A reading age of 9.05 is seen as sufficient for mastery of reading skills with no further help required.

No information is included in the Manual to indicate the origins of the Tests and there is no evidence of reliability or validity studies being carried out. This omission should not be taken to imply that no such work was done as J.C. Daniels is the author of a number of works on research methods and test construction. While this battery of tests has been carefully compiled in relation to basic decoding and comprehension skills, care should be taken that its interpretation is restricted. Pupils with reading ages of 9.05 years may well be presented with material which causes severe difficulties in reading across the curriculum, contrary to the information which is given in the Manual.

Since the original publication of this book of tests, much more awareness has grown of the need to give attention to reading development and extension throughout the curriculum. Contemporary theories of reading also stress linguistic and contextual processes in reading in addition to the visual and phonic aspects. Therefore, while this may be a useful approach for screening pupils entering the secondary stage of education (for which it is often used) a wider diagnosis of reading abilities would be more appropriate.

Finally, some comment on the use of Test 12 should be made. This test is widely used as a standardized attainment measure, often for no better reason than the low cost with which copies can be reproduced. However, the reservations that have been expressed about sentence completion in previous reviews also apply here. Moreover, Test 12 is technically and typographically perhaps among the least satisfactory of such tests.

Swansea Test of Phonic Skills

Phillip Williams

1981

**Schools Council Publications,
160 Great Portland Street, London W1N 6LL**

Group or Individual; Objective; Standardized; Children with Reading Ages less than 7.06; Equivalent Southgate Reading Ages; Untimed (approximately 40 minutes); Consumable; UK.

The Swansea Test is primarily intended as a diagnostic instrument for the provision of information about a child's relative strengths and weaknesses in phonic skills.

The test consists of 65 groups of five nonsense words. The tester reads out one of these words which must be circled by the child. The items cover five areas of phonics (short vowels, long vowels, initial letter blends, final letter blends and a 'miscellaneous' section). Scores from individual sub-tests can be interpreted to show strengths and weaknesses in phonic ability in order to guide choice of content in an individual reading programme. Total scores may be converted into Southgate reading ages up to 7.06 years.

Standardization was undertaken with a sample of 378 children with reading ages between 5.09 and 7.09, in three schools within an English LEA, and three schools within a Welsh LEA. Reliability coefficients during feasibility studies in 1967/8 ranged from .93 to .87 for the five sub-tests. Validation studies against 'similar' tests were not possible since none were in common use, but a correlation between this test and *Southgate Group Reading Test 1* (q.v.) of .78 is given.

In certain remedial settings there may be merits in deliberately measuring phonic 'knowledge' without reference to processes naturally used in reading, such as sight vocabulary, contextual cues and grammatical structure. However, this is a premise that many reading specialists would dispute. One could place more confidence in the validity of the test if there were evidence that it provides a sound practical basis for remedial work or that it gives teachers guidance of a sort not available from other tests which employ meaningful word recognition tasks.

Tests of Proficiency in English

National Foundation for Educational Research

1973

NFER-NELSON

Group (Reading, Listening and Writing), Individual (Speaking); Objective (Listening and Reading); Junior Children (especially non-native speakers of English); Untimed; Raw Scores ('Content-Referenced': convertible to levels of proficiency); Untimed; Consumable; UK.

This battery of tests is intended primarily for assessing the level of language skill in non-native speakers of English in junior schools. It is also suitable for native English-speaking children. Specified uses are placement, diagnosis and progress monitoring. The tests were developed by an NFER research team sponsored by the DES.

The tests amount to a substantial and comprehensive package, but the general organization is fairly simple: three main levels of skill are tested in each of the four language skill areas.

Listening

Level 1 (33 items). Selection of pictures to match short spoken statements.

Level 2 (28 items). Selection of pictures to match oral (tape recorded) material.

Level 3 (14 and 16 items). Multiple-choice comprehension tests of short passages (passages and questions are tape-recorded).

Speaking

Level 1 (25 items). Naming pictorially-represented activities.

Level 2 (35 items). Production of phrases, sentences or questions appropriate for characters portrayed in simple picture sequences.

Level 3 (11 items). Completion of sentences spoken by tester, description of pictorial episodes and continuation of a narrative.

Reading

Level 1 (33 items). Matching of pictures with written statements.

Level 2 (28 items). More complex picture – written language matching.

Level 3 (15 items). Multiple-choice continuous prose test.

Writing

Level 1 (25 items). Production of written words to match pictured objects and activities.

Level 2 (20 items). More advanced picture-description and sentence-completion tasks.

Level 3 (11 items). More advanced sentence-completion and production of extended writing on one of three essay titles.

Separate **test booklets** or **answer sheets** are used for each level and skill and there is a separate **Manual of Instructions** for each skill area. It would thus be possible to carry out testing in only one skill area without purchasing all the materials. Extensive use is made of pictorial material depicting children of Asian, oriental and West Indian origin. The Listening and Reading items are all multiple-choice but the tests of Speaking and Writing require the marker to judge intelligibility and analyse language output according to the number of 'T-units' produced. A T-unit is defined as 'one main clause plus any subordinate clauses related to it'. The amount of work this would involve, particularly for the Speaking tests, would be considerable.

A **General Guide** discusses the overall rationale of the battery and describes the linguistic and skill content of each sub-test in detail. This could be valuable in making precise analyses of the linguistic development of a learner of English as a second language. No conventional 'norms' are given for the tests. Interpretation is 'content-referenced', meaning that a learner's performance is to be interpreted in terms of the level of linguistic sophistication so far attained. Linguistic and pictorial content of tests is shared across skill areas so that some further diagnosis of discrepancies between modes of language may be possible.

Various internal-consistency reliability values are given for the Listening and Reading tests. These generally exceed .80 and are probably acceptable, given the brevity of some of the tests. A study of inter-marker agreement for the Speaking and Listening tests is reported which indicated a high level of agreement (correlations of .85 to .98) although this was limited to two markers working on 50 scripts only.

The tests were developed at a time when there was

considerable concern about the language problems of the children of recent immigrants to the UK. It seems likely that the relevance of such a test battery to the current needs of multi-racial schools is limited. However, the *Tests of Proficiency in English* remain one of the few purpose-designed means of assessing the capabilities of overseas children entering British junior schools. The battery is also very thorough, although the amount of work involved in their use could be formidable. It is possible to speculate that if the development of such a test were to be undertaken in 1983 rather than in 1973 a more sophisticated model of language would be adopted. For example, the concept of 'listening' and 'speaking' as separate skills is rather simplistic. However, in the early 1970s the tests were certainly a reasonable first attempt at a difficult task.

Thackray Reading Readiness Profiles

Derek and Lucy Thackray

1974 (Fifth impression 1981)

Hodder & Stoughton

Small Group or Individual; Objective; Standardized; 5.00 (soon after school entry); A-E Scale; Untimed (Profile 1, 20 minutes, Profile 2, 20 minutes, Profile 3, 20 minutes, Profile 4, 10 minutes); Consumable; UK.

These Reading Readiness Profiles are designed to provide the busy teacher with a quick measure of abilities and skills which are required for the child to learn to read easily and profitably.

All four Profiles are contained in one **test booklet** and measure the skills which the authors found to be the most important to readiness for reading.

Profile 1, Vocabulary and Concept Development (23 items), uses words based on young children's experiences. The child selects from the pictures the one that illustrates the word the tester gives.

Profile 2, Auditory Discrimination (17 items) measures the child's ability to discriminate between words which do or do not begin with the same initial consonants. Objects which are familiar to children are illustrated for the child to select as above.

Profile 3, Visual Discrimination (27 items) requires the child to select matching words from a choice of four. The size of print is gradually reduced from 36-point to 24-point.

Profile 4, General Ability uses a revised version of the *Goodenough Draw-a-Man Test*. The child is instructed to draw a picture of its mother. This is then graded on a five-point scale by comparing the drawing with five sets of definitive examples.

The **Manual of Instructions** gives very straightforward instructions for administration of the tests which must be followed exactly if valid results are to be obtained. Also included are descriptions of the nature and purpose of the profiles, instructions for scoring, data relating to development and activities to foster reading readiness skills.

Scores are interpreted into five ratings, A–E, with B, C and D each approximately one standard deviation in width. A and E are beyond 1.5 standard deviations above and below the mean respectively. In effect, the scores place children in broad general categories. The results are recorded in a five-column profile on the cover of the pupil's test booklet.

The Profiles were published after 10 years of research in order to indicate areas of pre-reading activities which will help to prepare children to learn to read. Standardization took place in 1973, with 5,500 children drawn from 350 schools representing urban and rural areas in England, Scotland, Wales and N. Ireland. Ages ranged from 4.08 to 5.08 years, averaging 5.00. The children had started school in September and had been in school about six weeks at the time of assessment. Reliability coefficients of .80, .81 and .90 for Profiles 1, 2 and 3 were computed by split-half technique. This is a form of internal consistency measure. Validity coefficients between Profiles 1, 2 and 3 with achievement test scores a year later ranged between 0.45 and 0.58 (using Southgate, Schonell and Neale tests). Scores for the four Profiles were found to be moderately inter-correlated. These results indicated that although the tests overlap to some extent, all four are needed for a full evaluation of a child's reading readiness abilities.

The Profiles are fairly time-consuming in that they require four sessions which will need to be spread over more than one day. Time is also required for the teacher to be thoroughly prepared and conversant with the contents and exact mode of administration. Great care would have to be taken to ensure that the children tested were sophisticated enough to cope with the activities required, such as underlining and following verbal instructions. One useful purpose which these Profiles might serve would be to demonstrate to anxious parents clear reasons why a child had not yet started on a formal reading programme. On the other hand, in no way should results be used as a reason to neglect the child's development in early reading skills.

TOP (Testing Our Pupils)

1976

The Open University

Group and Individual tests; Some Objective; Some Standardized; Top Infant-Lower Junior; Some Re-usable parts; UK.

TOP is a diagnostic battery of tests assembled in Block 10, Folder Material, of the Open Univeristy *Personality and Learning* Course E201. The materials are primarily intended as *examples* of tests for use with children with learning difficulties. Nevertheless, the materials cover many major features of reading difficulty and it would be entirely practical to prepare the battery for routine use.

The materials were developed for a remedial programme in the London Borough of Barnet and are comprised as follows:

1. Carver's *Word Recognition Test* (q.v.). A modified scoring system is used, based on stencils which allow error patterns to be classified as reflecting either auditory confusion, consonant cluster errors, letter sequencing difficulty or visual confusion.

2. The *English Picture Vocabulary Test*. This is a well-established standardized test of vocabulary. The latest version of the test is available from NFER-NELSON.

3. Problem of Position (POP). The child must join sets of up to four dots, embedded in a larger group to match a target set of dots, printed adjacently. There are 25 items, printed in a separate test booklet.

4. Please Avoid Wrong Sequence (PAWS). This is a visual sequential memory test, similar to the one used in the *Aston Index* (q.v.). PAWS involves picture matching. Five increasingly long sequences of pictures of animals must be reproduced, using separate card pictures of the animals.

5. Letter Memory Span (LMS). Twelve letter strings are read aloud by the tester and the child must repeat each correctly.

6. Discrimination of Phonemes (DOP). The child is asked whether particular sounds can be heard in each of 12 words spoken by the tester, e.g. "Can you hear "m" in jug?". In six cases the target sounds are present in the word.

7. Blending of Phonemes (BOP). Twenty sound blending tasks are presented in which words are enunciated letter by letter and the child must blend the sounds to reproduce the word.

Both DOP and BOP are pre-recorded on a **cassette.**

8. Word Retention (WR). Two words are printed on polyart paper so they are visible when held to the light but disappear when the paper is laid flat. The child must study the words by holding up the sheet and then endeavour to write them out from memory.

Test performance is recorded on a separate **record form** and there is also a **pupil profile** sheet for summarizing performance, using a 'Weak/Average/Strong' classification. The testing procedures are fully outlined in a **Test Booklet** which includes a 'provisional' scoring guide based on results for 400 backward readers.

Technical information on TOP is limited, although an internal consistency coefficient of .93 is given for POP and it is noted some, but not all, the tests had proved valid predictors of reading progress.

The folder of materials includes a 15-page **Remedial Activities Booklet** which discusses procedures for remediating weaknesses in the skills covered in the TOP tests.

As TOP is intended primarily to exemplify diagnostic procedures it might be inappropriate to consider it as a finally worked-out procedure intended for routine use. Even so, it contains ideas which teachers could profitably use and which have been influential in the development of other diagnostic procedures, notably the *Barking Reading Project* materials (q.v.).

Warwickshire Literacy Placement Guide

J.E. Mount and Aubrey C. Nichols

1976

NARE

Individual; Objective; Unstandardized; Adult; Untimed; Re-usable; UK.

The Guide is intended for initial diagnostic assessment of new adult literacy students. The authors also refer to a possible place for the Guide in secondary education.

Both the instructions and tests are printed in a 16-page **booklet.** There are five sub-tests:

Social Sight Vocabulary. Thirteen words, such as 'down', 'up' and 'danger' are presented both in large print and in pictorial contexts.

Key Words. The 32 most frequent of McNally and Murray's *Keywords to Literacy* are printed in the squares of a large grid.

Continuous Prose. A narrative is printed in five sections on successive pages. The sections are graded in difficulty and the instructions suggest, not at all clearly, that these can be cross referenced with lists of graded reading material.

Letter Names and Sounds. Letters of the alphabet printed in upper and lower case to be named and sounded by the student.

Phonic Conventions. This consists of word recognition lists covering some 15 elementary aspects of phonics.

The Introduction explains that the Guide was developed from an experimental version produced in 1975 but it is not claimed that any of the conventional validation or standardization procedures have been carried out. The original intention was, evidently, to develop the Placement Guide through practical experience using the experimental version in adult literacy teaching. Sadly, very little of this practical value is conveyed in the two explanatory pages of 'Suggestions for Administration', which read like notes on the main text of the experimental version. Indeed, the actual procedures for giving the tests are far from clear. Users of the materials might be able to improvise their own testing procedures using the printed test pages, but beyond this, the *Warwickshire Literacy Placement Guide* would seem to be of little use in assessing adult literacy learners. Literacy, in any case, includes writing ability, a matter not covered in the Guide. Overall, the approach taken by Holmes and Good in *How's It Going?* (q.v.) offers a more comprehensive and sensitive means of assessment in the adult literacy field.

Word Recogniton Test

Clifford Carver

1970

Hodder & Stoughton

Group or Individual; Objective; Standardized; Up to 8.06; Word Recognition Ages; Untimed (15–30 minutes); Consumable; UK.

The Carver Test is intended to give an overall measure of word recognition ability and to permit analysis of patterns and categories of error and difficulty. The author recommends the test for use in large-scale surveys, screening, recording progress (here the absence of equivalent forms of the test would be a disadvantage), research and diagnosis of 'perceptual errors in word recognition'.

The test has 50 items. A stimulus word is read out by the teacher and the child must locate the word amongst five or six alternatives printed in rows in the test booklet. Some of the alternatives are nonsense words, others are real English words. Raw score totals are converted to Word Recognition Ages using a simple table of norms. These age scores correspond to ten stages of word recognition which are outlined in detail in a further table in the 25-page **Manual of Instructions.** These stages allow what amounts to a criterion-referenced interpretation of the child's score. They are based on the author's research which showed a systematic pattern in the order in which letters are 'learned'. However, Carver stresses that the stages are 'broad structures' based on average performances and cannot be expected to apply in detail to any individual child. Variations in teaching in the early stages might well upset the 'natural order' of these stages.

The Manual discusses further diagnostic assessment in some detail. It advises the teacher to take account of chronological age, word recognition level, pattern of correct responses, and pattern of errors. The back cover of the test booklet contains a table for recording errors in ten general categories reflecting aural and visual aspects of word and letter manipulation. Earlier it is noted that the wrong answer alternatives were designed to cover the ten categories of error. However, a detailed and explicit cross-classification of items and categories is not provided. It would appear that during the development of the test a division into six 'sub-tests' was employed but this was dropped from the published version. Thus, the effectiveness of diagnosis would depend greatly upon the teacher's willingness to systematically analyse and interpret children's wrong answers on an item-by-item basis. A tally of different categories of error would be technically possible, but would be time consuming to carry out for more than a few children. However, the TOP materials (q.v.) contain an example of an overlay key designed to facilitate diagnostic scoring of this particular test.

Details of the development, validation and standardization are given at some length, but the account is not always easy to follow. It would appear that the test was initially developed in an intensive study with 148 children and subsequently standardized on 1005 children. Reference is also made to further research with Canadian children. Reliability of the test would appear to be very high and substantial correlations with both published word recognition tests and experimental measures are quoted. The extent to which the norms for the test are based on representative samples of children is not explained, but it can be argued that precision in this respect is not crucial for classroom use of the test. However, the Carver happens to be popular for large-scale screening in some LEAs, where normative considerations may carry greater weight.

As a test of word recognition the Carver goes far beyond other such tests in providing a constructive analysis of word reading skills. It is therefore a pity that the test stops short of systematic guidance on error analysis and classification. The author is properly cautious in stressing the relevance of the test is limited in age range 'up to about 8 years and 6 months' and no claims are made for its use beyond that of establishing how far a 'sound structured basis to word recognition has developed'.

Section III: Checklists

Materials reviewed in this section exemplify different ways in which checklists can be used in appraisal of reading and reading difficulty. Checklists lack the statistical refinement and objectivity of formal tests. However, they have the potential to alert teachers to important questions which are not amenable to testing because of various practical constraints. All too often reviews in Sections I and II have contained reservations about the underlying model of reading or simplistic assumptions on which tests are based. In this respect checklists offer a positive alternative, although it could be said that tests measure unimportant things thoroughly while checklists measure important things superficially. In fact, the value of using a checklist will depend largely upon the knowledge, insight and observational skill of the teacher and the thoughtfulness with which the checklist is completed.

The reviews are confined to commercially published examples. However, one of the advantages of checklists is the ease with which teachers can make their own. The most interesting examples are probably in local use in schools and LEAs. Some of those reviewed here might be treated as prototypes for adaptation or patterns for creating checklists to cover aspects of reading – of which there are many – not tackled in any published materials.

The checklist approach may also appeal to teachers with principled objections to testing children who nevertheless need to carry out systematic assessments.

Aston Portfolio

Carol Aubrey, Jane Eaves, Carlyn Hicks and
Margaret Newton

1981 (approximately)

LDA

The Portfolio consists of a **boxed set of cards** and **checklists** for assessing and teaching children with reading and writing difficulties. The materials are recommended for classroom use, as well as in more specialized remedial settings. Equal attention is given to both the process of assessing and diagnosing and follow-up teaching. The Portfolio is perhaps unique amongst British-developed teaching aids in the weight it attaches to initial assessment.

Assessment commences with completion of a checklist covering 18 aspects of spelling, 25 aspects of reading and four aspects of written expression. This is done by reference to questions printed on three **Assessment Cards.** These are used to identify skills that a child may not have mastered, to be noted on the cover of an individual four-page **Assessment Checklist,** supplied in multiple copies. The next three pages specify performance sub-tests for all the skills itemized on the Checklist Assessment Cards. The teacher can thus carry these out to verify the initial judgements. This serves to partly validate the checklist, although no account is taken of deficits overlooked at the initial stage.

The Portfolio's analysis of language learning emphasizes initial skills. Spelling is sub-categorized into a series of Auditory, Visual and Auditory-Visual Skills. Reading follows a similar pattern but includes Advanced Reading Skills – based mainly on cloze procedure tests. The written expression sub-tests focus initially on spoken language and descriptive and narrative skills in sentence writing.

Alongside each sub-test, reference is made to corresponding **Teaching Cards** in the Portfolio. These are organized into six main groups, identified by colour:

Reading (Visual and Auditory Skills)
Spelling
Reading and Spelling Appendix (dictation exercises)
Handwriting
Comprehension
Written Expression

The Teaching Cards contain over 500 teaching ideas from which individual remedial programmes can be developed. The 26-page **Handbook** stresses that it is up to the teacher to use this 'market place of ideas' to develop a teaching programme, although further advice is given on planning and organizing the work, together with illustrative examples.

Thirty copies of a **Handwriting Checklist** are supplied with the Portfolio. This was developed independently of the main materials by Jean Alston and is accompanied by its own instruction booklet. The Handwriting Checklist covers 23 main aspects of handwriting including motor skills and details of letter formation, and is completed by reference to samples of the child's written work.

There is also provision for using results previously obtained from the *Aston Index* (q.v.) as an alternative to the Assessment Cards for initial diagnosis. A special **Aston Index Assessment Card** is included in the Portfolio which cross references *Aston Index* tests with Assessment Checklist sub-tests.

The Portfolio, like the *Aston Index,* is a result of work by the Language Development Unit at Aston University. No formal claims for conventional validity and reliability are made, but thorough practical and experimental work preceded the publication of the Portfolio and post-publication trials are continuing.

The Portfolio is elaborate, by design, and would require time to be spent on basic familiarization before it could be used. This would be well worthwhile, particularly for those undertaking remedial work for the first time or with limited supporting resources. Less experienced teachers would certainly learn much about the nature of language difficulties in the course of using the materials, apart from any practical help they might be giving their pupils. In fact, the Portfolio has great potential as a training device in both initial and in-service work. Perhaps its most outstanding feature is avoidance of 'de-skilling' the teacher: the materials are detailed and structured, but ultimately they build professional skill rather than replace it. In this respect the Portfolio is in a different league to many boxed kits of remedial workcards.

Given the ambitious scope of the Portfolio minor flaws are unavoidable. In particular, the treatment of written expression and advanced comprehension has a less extensive research base on which to draw. Also, the value of recommending the *Neale Analysis of Reading Ability* (q.v.) as a comprehension check might be disputed. Nevertheless, the Aston Portfolio is a promising published solution to the problem of integrating diagnosis and teaching.

Dyslexia Schedule and School Entrance Check List

John McLeod

1969

Better Books

The materials consist of individual questionnaires for use with parents of children who have reading difficulties, or for screening at school entry for diagnostic purposes.

The *Dyslexia Schedule* contains 81 questions asking for information from the parent about physical, developmental and social characteristics relating to the child and the family. The *School Entrance Check List* is a shorter version of 18 questions which are intended to be 'less impertinent' and are recorded as 'yes' or 'no' responses.

The areas covered by the questionnaires were determined by examination of literature (listed in the bibliography in the 14-page **Manual**) and selecting characteristics listed by one or more of the authors. This was augmented by data obtained from twenty children who had been referred to the Remedial Education Centre of the University of Queensland, Australia, because of reading difficulties. Twenty children in a control group had the schedule completed for them, and, from these data, 16 out of the original 90 items were found to discriminate significantly between the two groups. A further try-out was undertaken using an amended version, with 23 children from Grade Two in Brisbane schools, with a similar control group. This time 23 items showed statistically significant discrimination. No results of predictive validation are available.

We are forced to question why this schedule has ever been published, and to what purpose it is intended to relate. Psychologists or teachers using the schedule would be ill-advised to classify children as dyslexic on the basis of the limited validity evidence noted above. A much more thorough and wide ranging validation exercise would be needed before the routine use of such a schedule could be justified.

Framework for Reading

Joan Dean and Ruth Nichols

1974

Evans Brothers, Montague House, Russell Square, London WC1B 5BX

Framework for Reading is a 95-page handbook on both the early teaching and remediation of reading. A major feature of the book is two sets of comprehensive checklists. These are designed for recording individual progress in the early primary years and remedial diagnosis of difficulty in somewhat older pupils. They are also available in **spirit master** form for local duplication. The checklists are intended for ordinary classroom use, rather than with children who have special or severe language difficulties.

Check List 1 focuses on the knowledge and skills required in beginning and early reading and is divided into six major sections:

A. The Language of Instruction
B. Reading Skills, Level 1 Word Recognition
C. Handwriting Skills
D. The Analysis of Word Patterns, Phonic Knowledge, Level 1
E. Development of Reading Skills, Level 2
F. Phonic Knowledge, Level 2

The checklist should be used to obtain a cumulative record of progress using a combination of direct testing, observation and summary appraisals. Completion of the Checklist would thus take place in the course of many weeks of teaching. The teacher is then encouraged to review progress through the skills checked and make a summary of auditory, linguistic, sequencing or visual difficulties which may have emerged. Chapter 4 of the handbook discusses practical teaching activities which can be applied to develop the skills covered in the checklist. There is thus a thorough cross referencing of assessment and teaching advice.

Check List 2 is for children whose progress is felt to be unsatisfactory and is divided into five main sections:

G. Motivation and attitudes
H. Child's understanding of language
I. Child's own use of language
J. Auditory factors
K. Vision and visual factors

Sections J and K contain 13 sub-sections covering most of the main cognitive and physical factors associated with reading difficulty. Chapter 6 of the handbook is a systematic discussion of remedial strategies appropriate to each section of Check List 2.

Careful recording of progress is important in the early stages of learning to read and *Framework for Reading* provides a valuable structure for this. In practice, teachers may prefer to regard the two checklists as models to be condensed or used selectively. Certainly, it would be necessary to search far to find a materially better model of good practice or a sounder account of early literacy development on which to base a teacher-made monitoring system. The emphasis upon the inter-relatedness of reading, writing, spoken language and motor and perceptual skills is particularly welcome. In effect, *Framework for Reading* equips the teacher with a coherent curriculum guide as well as a means of assessment and diagnosis. It is well worth considering as an alternative to formal testing.

How's It Going?

Martin Good and John Holmes

1978

**Adult Literacy Unit
(order from Interprint Graphic Services Ltd,
Half Moon Street, Bagshot, Surrey)**

Individual; Unstandardized; Adult; Untimed; UK; Handbook on assessment using tutor-made checklists.

In *Reading : How To* (Penguin, 1974) Herbert Kohl, the radical American educationalist describes a checklist, in the form of a grid, which may be used to rate progress in learning to read. Kohl suggests that reading can be regarded as developing through four levels, 'Beginning', 'Not Bad', 'With Ease' and 'Complex'. These levels define horizontal dimensions of the grid. At each level there are skills to be learned and matters of confidence, strategy, speed, stamina and understanding to be tackled; these constitute vertical dimensions. In *How's It Going?* the authors develop some of the main features of Kohl's scheme to provide 'an alternative to testing students in adult literacy'. Their purpose is to give the adult literacy student, as well as the tutor, general insights into what is involved in being, or becoming, literate, and to create a means for evaluating individual progress.

How's It Going? is a 77-page handbook addressed to both tutor *and* learner. It has much to say about the nature of literacy and its teaching, as well as the criteria by which progress can be judged. Particular emphasis is placed upon overcoming misconceptions about the nature of literacy and the sense of defeat and inadequacy which new adult literacy students often exhibit. The central component is a pair of charts/ checklists for reading and writing. These use Kohl's first three levels to assess progress in 20 diverse aspects of reading and 19 aspects of writing. These are categorized as either attitudes, skills or knowledge and the precise meaning of each is discussed in the handbook. These are graded on the basis of 'knows it', 'is working at it' or 'hasn't started yet'. Thus, precise judgements of the learner's capabilities can be made over a wide range of items. However, the authors stress that the charts are not immutable, and encourage users to make their own changes as seem necessary.

No claims are made for the reliability or validity of judgements based on the checklists. Much would depend upon the thoroughness with which the handbook is studied and the skill and experience of the tutor. Indeed, it would be hard to employ the checklists properly without close consideration of what the authors have to say about them. It would also be necessary to accept the framework which Holmes and Good use to analyse progress in literacy. Given these conditions there is no reason to believe that acceptable levels of reliability and validity could not be attained.

The handbook is an important contribution to diagnostic assessment of literacy for a number of reasons. Active involvement of the learner in the process of assessment is a valuable innovation which deserves to be more widely practised. The conception of 'literacy' is a broad one which includes appreciation of the communicative nature of written language, use of libraries and development of study skills as well as traditional matters such as sight vocabulary and phonics. The prominence given to attitudes is also striking. Ten of the 20 reading chart items have an attitudinal dimension. Good and Holmes really use 'attitude' as a shorthand term for the learner's general orientation towards literacy. This includes overcoming fear of the written word and willingness to regard it as human in origin ('everything written was written by someone') and amenable to enjoyment and criticism. It is a term used also to include response to failure and includes 'failing well' and ability to cope with mistakes. It also includes willingness to use all available strategies to get meaning from print, rather than believing that only certain strategies are 'permissible'.

There would be problems in a diligent step-by-step application of the checklists as the exact sequence in which they are to be used is not always clear. It seems at some points that sets of criteria cut across one another and thoughtful prior study would be necessary to resolve possible confusions. However, this is a minor flaw in an otherwise outstanding example of a checklist-based approach to diagnostic assessment. Although the material is intended primarily for adult literacy teaching it contains much which is worth consideration by anyone concerned with remedial assessment. (If some form of annual 'prize' was awarded for reading tests *How's It Going?* would deserve to win it!)

Reading Readiness Inventory

John Downing and Derek Thackray

1976

Hodder & Stoughton

The Inventory is a **two-page leaflet** containing a series of 50 questions mainly requiring Yes/No answers concerning an individual child. The questions cover four main areas: Physiological Factors; Environmental Factors; Emotional, Motivational and Personality Factors; Intellectual Factors. In effect, the conventional headings under which reading 'readiness' is usually considered. The Inventory is not intended to be a validated instrument so much as a convenient recapitulation of material discussed at length in the authors' book *Reading Readiness* (Hodder & Stoughton, second edition, 1975). The aspects of development covered in the Inventory generally reflect established views relating to early reading covered in a number of standard published texts. However, it would be highly desirable – if not essential – to use the Inventory in conjunction with the authors' book. No separate manual or guide is published for the Inventory and a completed set of Yes/No answers would be of little use to anyone not familiar with the reasons for asking the questions and the implications the answers may have for teaching.

The questions themselves seem generally pertinent and are as free of ambiguity as is possible with such a device. In any case, some of the items in the Inventory, particularly those concerning cognitive, auditory and visual processes, raise questions in a simple form which are pursued in much greater depths in a number of formal performance tests, particularly the *Thackray Reading Readiness Profiles* (q.v.) and LARR (q.v.). The Inventory might be used as a preliminary indicator or to determine whether there is need for test-based follow-up of individual children. For example, the Inventory poses questions concerning the child's understanding of the purpose and organization of written language which are tested comprehensively in the LARR test. The Inventory also draws attention to less measurable, and perhaps less tractable, considerations of physique and family background.

There would be reasonable grounds in many infant and first schools for adopting this checklist, or something like it, as a routine part of a screening and record-keeping programme.

Section IV:
Spelling Tests

Much of the assessment of spelling which goes on in schools is based on informal tests devised by teachers. Certainly, standardized tests of spelling are less widely used than standardized reading tests and the choice of published tests is very limited. It may be that test producers have simply failed to appreciate the need or demand for properly developed and standardized spelling tests. One or two reading tests reviewed in Section I incorporate a spelling sub-test, notably Young's SPAR, *Cassell's Linked English Tests,* Daniels and Diack's *Standard Reading Tests* and *The Richmond Test of Basic Skills.* However, to more clearly reflect the complete range of spelling tests available – particularly those with a diagnostic emphasis – a number of further free-standing spelling tests should be considered. These are reviewed in this section.

Diagnostic and Remedial Spelling Manual

Margaret L. Peters

1979 (revised edition)

Macmillan Education

Group or Individual; Unstandardized; Ages 8.00–11.00; Untimed (approximately 45 minutes); No Equivalent Forms; Re-usable (Record Sheets available separately); UK.

The *Diagnostic and Remedial Spelling Manual* seeks to achieve the aims expressed in its title by qualitative analysis of spelling errors and emphasis on the importance of fostering autonomy in spelling. It particularly stresses the value of giving each child a successful spelling strategy and achieving a positive self-image of oneself as a good speller.

There have been some revisions in this second edition of the manual, mainly focusing on the categories in the *Spelling Record Sheet* appended to the manual. In her critique of spelling error classification schemes, Hazel Nelson (In: FRITH, U. (Ed.) (1980) *Cognitive Processes in Spelling.* Academic Press) points out that the quality of the information gained from an analysis of spelling errors is necessarily limited by the way in which the errors have been analysed, and she notes the difficulties of producing a system enabling all errors to be classified in a reliable way. It is worthy of note that the changes Dr. Peters has made in this revised version have been the result of much correspondence with teachers and students using the manual. In the original version there were many sub-categories analysing word structure which have largely been omitted from the second edition, on the basis that these yield little diagnostic information. Certainly, the procedure of recording errors is made much easier and less time-consuming in the light of these changes.

The test consists of three graded dictation passages, each of which are 100 words in length and intended for age groups 8.00–9.00; 9.00–10.00 and 10.00–11.00. The passage is delivered to the children in the traditional way, being firstly read in its entirety, then phrase-by-phrase and finally in its entirety once more.

The third section of the manual gives a more detailed account of each error category with practical suggestions for remediation. General teaching guidelines are covered including the familiar 'look, cover, write, check' routine.

Included in the manual are two further appendices. One gives the spelling ages of each word from the dictation passages and the other is a flow chart for a first or remedial spelling programme.

There are no reliability or validity data included in the manual. More background can be found in Peters' *Success in Spelling* (Cambridge Institute of Education, 1970) which gives a detailed account of the research project from which this manual arises. Since this is a criterion-referenced test no norms are provided and no spelling ages presented.

For each child the errors made in the dictation passage are recorded on the Spelling Record Sheet in the most appropriate of the five categories. A left-to-right procedure is suggested when recording these words – if an error does not fit into the first category it is tried in the second, and so on. The categories are as follows:

I. Reasonable phonic alternatives, including homophones (e.g. 'cote' for 'coat')

II. Unreasonable phonic alternatives, including transpositions (e.g. 'friend' for 'frightened' or 'siad' for 'said'

III. Faulty auditory perception or articulation (e.g. 'soud' for 'sound')

IV. Handwriting errors including perseveration (e.g. 'bark' for 'dark')

V. Unclassified errors (e.g. 'galte' for 'galloped')

When the errors have all been recorded, the teacher is able to tell fairly swiftly how serious the child's spelling problem is – clusters of errors to the right of the Record Sheet indicate a more severe problem than do clusters to the left. It is possible to tell if a child is on the way to becoming a competent speller even if at first the number of errors appears high. The information gained is sufficient to indicate to the teacher the most suitable remedial action.

The Diagnostic Dictation passages occupy only a small part of the manual. The rest concerns itself with issues such as the importance of a *diagnostic* test in spelling, spelling strategies, and teaching guidelines, all of which are very valuable. Far from being simply a spelling test, the manual embodies in 40 pages a complete and concise approach to the teaching of spelling.

Diagnostic Spelling Test

Denis Vincent and Jenny Claydon

1982

NFER-NELSON

Group; Objective; Standardized; 7.08–11.08; Mainly Untimed (70 minutes); Standardized Scores; Equivalent Forms (2) Consumable; UK.

This test, consisting of a dictation and seven sub-tests, sets out to identify poor spellers by examining their performance in sub-skills that underpin good spelling. These sub-tests are as follows:

1. The ability to distinguish *homophones,* i.e. the exploration of the link between visual pattern and meaning.

2. The ability to spell *common words,* the items being based on clearly illustratable nouns found in *Words Your Children Use* (R.P.A. Edwards and V. Gibbon).

3. *Proof Reading* tests the capacity to rapidly identify words that do not 'look right'.

4. *Letter Strings* focuses on the recognition of regular spelling patterns and the ability to build on it.

5. *Nonsense Words* investigates knowledge of probabilities and the frequency with which given letters are sequenced to form strings.

6. *Dictionary Use* checks on one commonly recommended means of monitoring spelling.

7. The *Self-Concept* checklist identifies pupils who lack a positive image of themselves as spellers.

The *100-word dictation* measures overall spelling ability of a passage of continuous prose.

Raw scores for the whole range of sub-tests are recorded on the **pupil's booklet** and converted to a standardized score. The clear and concise **Teacher's Guide** gives an account of the reliability and validity studies carried out, and a further report on this aspect is in preparation.

The reviewer has administered the *Diagnostic Spelling Test* in a strictly diagnostic setting to children with acknowledged learning problems, aged 7.00+ to 14.00+. The immediately noticeable feature was that scores achieved by pupils on this new test keep in step with their performance on Young's *SPAR* (q.v.) test and the Peters' Diagnostic Dictation in the *Diagnostic and Remedial Spelling Manual* (q.v.). Scores on the *Diagnostic Spelling Test* were unaffected by starting or finishing with the dictation, which, for level of difficulty, is close to the Peters' dictation for age 7.00–8.00. Children whose oral reading was stuck at the mechanical stage obtained a maximum of half marks on the nonsense words sub-test. The ones who had low scores on the letter strings sub-test invariably failed to use systematic scanning, although some had well-practised cursive writing. Poor recall of common words did not, according to school exercise books, necessarily inhibit free writing; on being questioned these children explained that 'teacher/my friend tells me' how to spell a word, or that they just did not worry, free writing being seen as something of an occasion for a fine careless rapture. The self-concept checklist revealed all the younger children to be confused about whether they were careful or careless spellers. This suggests that practices constituting a careful speller need to be specifically demonstrated.

The sub-tests examine a number of closely related, substantially visual skills, but there is no mention of their dependence on visual sequential memory. The choice of tasks examined would evoke support from teachers, although the details of sub-tests might be open to question: for instance, in the proofreading sub-test none of the miscues involve the order of letters nor the omission of audible vowels. In fact all the miscues are reasonable or near-reasonable phonic alternatives, the most advanced category. This chimes in with the general level of the test which indicates the directions in which spelling proficiency can be buffed up, rather than give an order of priority for teaching the pupil whose spelling has barely got off the ground.

The *Diagnostic Spelling Test* develops the work of Peters by adding task-based analysis to the familiar miscue analysis, which concentrates on spelling as the finished product of dictation. Teachers will welcome the test because by identifying sub-skills it also defines teaching objectives which can easily be pursued both in the classroom and in remedial sessions. As such, it is an aid to precision teaching. In a diagnostic setting, as one of a battery of tests, it will be particularly useful in refining the description of learning disability and consequently again leading to precision in advice for remediation.

Diagnostic Spelling Tests

Gill Cotterell

(undated)

LDA

Individual (or small group); Unstandardized; Untimed; 9.00+ to adult; Re-usable; UK.

The tests described in this 16-page **handbook** are intended to provide a simple means of diagnosing spelling problems at any level, including adult and higher education. It is particularly recommended that they are used in conjunction with the author's *Check List of Basic Sounds* and *Phonic Reference Cards*.

The Tests consist of lists of target words and are accompanied by various practical suggestions for follow-up work. The Tests represent four levels of learning to spell.

Level 1, (Tests 1a, 1b, 1c, 1d). Early phonics and spelling rules.

Level 2, (Tests 2a, 2b, 2c). More advanced phonics and spelling rules.

Level 3, (Tests 3a, 3b, 3c). Polysyllables, wider range of prefixes and suffixes, harder phonic structure and spelling rules.

Level 4, (Tests 4a, 4b, 4c). Words and patterns which give particular trouble to weak spellers, including GCE candidates.

The order of the Tests represents a rough progression in learning. Teachers are advised not to give more than two tests in a session, unless the pupil is able to spell nearly all the words tested, as each list represents as much as a term's work for a poor speller.

A key principle in the teaching of spelling is that it should be systematic and this short booklet certainly introduces the teacher to a systematic approach. The materials have the added strength of having been developed out of the author's extensive practical experience. However, there are limitations in the focus on spelling as a 'phonic' process in the way recommended in the booklet. It is assumed that materials and approaches primarily intended for teaching reading will be equally applicable to spelling. This is misleading, as a comparison with Margaret Peters' *Diagnostic and Remedial Spelling Manual* (q.v.) should show. Successful spelling involves the development of effective strategies for spelling more than the systematic 'overlearning' of particular phonic elements, as recommended in this booklet. The best way to use these tests would be alongside the approaches recommended in Dr. Peters' manual.

Schonell Graded Word Spelling Tests A and B

Fred Schonell

1955

Oliver & Boyd

Group; Objective; Standardized; 5.00–15.00; Spelling Ages; Untimed; Equivalent Forms (2); Re-usable; UK.

Each form of this test consists of a list of 100 words graded in difficulty and printed in groups of ten on the teacher's **test sheet.** Each word is read aloud by the teacher who must devise a simple context sentence to indicate its meaning. The words are to be written by pupils on a sheet of paper. Ideally, testing should start with the group of words judged to match the general level of group ability and continue until eight to ten words have been failed. This is easier to secure when testing individually.

For every word spelled correctly the pupil is credited with a tenth of a year in spelling age, commencing at 5.00 years. It is possible to convert scores to spelling quotients using a simple formula.

The tests have been in regular use since 1955 – mainly because few alternative standardized measures are available – but no re-standardization has been carried out and their normative accuracy must surely be open to question. Young's *SPAR* test (q.v.) probably provides a better alternative if a simple standardized word list test is required. In any case the value of testing spelling on the basis of an arbitrary list of words is questionable. The relationship of performance on such tests to accuracy of spelling in free-writing and non-test situations has not been demonstrated. Certainly, no reliability or validity information is offered for the Schonell tests. There may well be a valid need for standardized measures of spelling ability, particularly for screening of poor spellers and evaluating remedial progress. Nevertheless, it is highly debatable that these tests are adequate for such purposes and it is to be hoped more suitable instruments will eventually become available. In the meantime, no disservice will be done to pupils by teachers who decide to abandon the use of the Schonell spelling tests.

Appendix A: Cloze Procedure

A number of the tests reviewed employ 'cloze' procedure and this is becoming a popular technique for both formal and informal assessment of reading. Briefly, a cloze test is a prose passage which contains a number of blank spaces into which missing words must be written. The method was developed by Taylor (1953) who suggested that a reader had a tendency or 'gestalt' to complete or 'cloze' incomplete samples of written language. Cloze originally developed as a measure of readability of text but is now used in a number of ways, including measurement of reading comprehension.

Much research has been conducted into different ways of preparing cloze tests and applying them to different types of texts. Particular attention has been given to rules for deleting words and scoring the results. In readability research it is customary to automatically delete every fifth word in a passage but in comprehension testing a lower rate, between eight and ten, is more common. Comprehension tests also have to discriminate in selection of words to be deleted in order to control the difficulty of the test. Vincent and Cresswell (1976) suggest that a balanced test can be created for classroom use by deleting roughly *every* tenth word in a 100-word passage. Two or three of these should be simple structural words and the remainder content words. It should also be ensured that all the latter words *could* be discovered by use of context, either because they are used elsewhere in the passage or could reasonably be inferred.

Debate has also focused on methods of marking cloze tests. Purists claim that only the author's original words count as correct whereas others argue that synonyms reflecting understanding of content and sensitivity to style should be allowed. It is certainly easier to follow the exact replacement method as used by Bormuth (1968) and research studies seem to indicate that the verbatim method of scoring is just as valid as any other. In practice standardized cloze tests tend to contain items which do not invite many feasible alternatives. In marking such tests it is essential to follow exactly the scoring procedure laid down – however seemingly arbitrary – if norms are to be applied. In diagnostic use the question of correctness is less acute. McKenna (1976) quotes research studies which indicate the benefits of accepting a range of responses rather than only the author's original wording.

Cloze has generally been accepted as an improvement over word-recognition and sentence-completion testing. Standardized cloze tests can probably be used with as much confidence as any other form of test although much remains to be learned about the relationship between cloze procedure and reading ability.

References

BORMUTH, J.R. (1968). 'The Cloze readability procedure', *Elementary English,* 45, pp. 429-36.

McKENNA, M. (1976). 'Synonymic versus verbatim scoring of the Cloze Procedure', *Journal of Reading,* November, pp. 141-43.

TAYLOR, W.C. (1953). 'Cloze procedure: a new tool for measuring Readability', *Journalism Quarterly,* 30, pp. 415-33.

VINCENT, D. and CRESSWELL, M. (1976). *Reading Tests in the Classroom,* p. 121. NFER-NELSON.

Appendix B: Addresses of Main Test Publishers and Distributors

Better Books,
15a Chelsea Road,
Lower Weston, Bath BA1 3DU

Cassell Ltd,
35 Red Lion Square,
London WC1R 4SG

Educational Evaluation Enterprises,
Awre, Newnham, Gloucestershire GL14 1ET

Hart-Davis Educational,
Granada Publishing,
PO Box 9, 29 Frogmore,
St Albans, Hertfordshire AL2 2NF

Heinemann Educational,
22 Bedford Square,
London WC1B 3HH

Hodder & Stoughton Ltd,
PO Box 6, Mill Road,
Dunton Green, Sevenoaks,
Kent TN13 2XX

LDA, Duke Street, Wisbech,
Cambridgeshire PE13 2AE

Macmillan Education Ltd,
Houndsmill, Basingstoke,
Hampshire RG21 2XS

NFER-NELSON Publishing Company Ltd,
Darville House, 2 Oxford Road East,
Windsor, Berkshire SL4 1DF

Oliver & Boyd
(A Division of Longman Group Ltd.)
Robert Stevenson House,
1-3 Baxter's Place,
Leith Walk,
Edinburgh EH1 3AF

SRA, Newtown Road, Henley-on-Thames,
Oxon RG9 1EW

The Test Agency, Cournswood House,
North Dean, High Wycombe, Buckinghamshire

Index of Tests